EUREKA!

Build Communication Confidence and
Enhance Work Relationships

Simple Steps and Proven Solutions!

EUREKA!

Build Communication Confidence and
Enhance Work Relationships

Simple Steps and Proven Solutions!

Susan Langlitz, Ph.D.

Word Association Publishers
205 Fifth Avenue
Tarentum, Pennsylvania 15084

Copyright 2003 by Susan Langlitz, Ph.D.

All rights reserved. No part of this book may be used or reproduced in any manner whatsoever without written permission of the author.

Printed in the United States of America.

ISBN: 1-932205-84-5
Library of Congress Control Number: 2003115910

Word Association Publishers
205 Fifth Avenue,
Tarentum, Pennsylvania 15084
www.wordassociation.com

To *my father*

Acknowledgements

My grateful thanks to the following people who helped bring this book to fruition:

Susan Newhof, my editor for her patience, guidance, creativity, diplomacy, talent and friendship.

Valerie Lee Blane, my proofreader for her versatility, encouragement, precision, humor and generosity.

Stephen and Nikki Marks for their insight, creativity and pragmatism.

Julianne C. Waesche for the profound communication journey.

My family of origin, whom without all the joy, blessings, sorrow, magnificence and struggle, this book would never have been born.

Chapter One   **1**
"Everyone *Has A Story*" – *We all have trials and tribulations with others at work. This chapter provides a baseline for the rest of the book by helping the reader focus on his or her personal experiences and difficult patterns and the way we define ourselves.*

Chapter Two   **5**
"Why Do People Treat Me Like They Do?" – *Eye-opening insight as to why people act the way they do.*

Chapter Three   **16**
"How You Treat Yourself Is Most Important" – *How others treat us is often reflected in how we treat ourselves and feel about ourselves. This chapter encourages the reader to take action and make choices that will result in growth and empowerment.*

Chapter Four   **22**
"You Have To Be Willing To Take a Risk" – *Concrete steps on how to move forward that begins with a personal inventory of communication skills.*

Chapter Five   **31**
"Four Steps To Bridge The Communication Gap" – *Four steps that anyone can practice at work.*

Chapter Six   **46**
"Confrontation Is Not A Four Letter Word" – *Methods for confronting others in a positive, non-defensive manner that will result in shared understanding and productive outcomes.*

Chapter Seven   **62**
"How Do I Get What I Want?" – *Practical ideas and steps for getting what we want from others at work.*

Chapter Eight **71**
"How Do I Handle Criticism? How Do I Give Others Feedback Without Hurting Their Feelings?" – *A step-by-step recipe for responding to others' criticism and giving others feedback in a professional, productive manner.*

Chapter Nine **83**
"How Do I Gain Respect And Credibility From Others?" – *Simple, practical steps to achieve this important goal.*

Chapter Ten **96**
"How Can I Be A Better Speaker And Gain a Sense of Confidence?" – *How to craft a presentation and deliver it in an interesting, engaging manner, as well as suggestions for enhancing and exuding confidence.*

Chapter Eleven **111**
"How Do I Know When It's Time To Leave A Situation, Job Or Relationship?" – *Answers to difficult questions that can help us decide when to stay in challenging situations and when to call it quits.*

PROLOGUE

I have taught, trained and spoken to people of all ages and walks of life for the past twenty years. For a long time, I pondered what to write about which would be helpful to you, my reader. Then, one day, it dawned on me. It was quite obvious – EUREKA!

Over the years, various individuals, groups and audiences have repeatedly, consistently asked me questions such as, why do people treat me the way they do? How do I handle criticism? How do I speak in front of people? How do I gain credibility and respect? How can I get what I want from others?

These questions are universal and transcend any particular group of people. This book includes those questions, among others, and my best responses from my own research, professional experience, and personal trials and tribulations.

Thank you for your inspiration and motivation to write this book. I hope it makes a difference for you.

Chapter One

EVERYONE HAS A STORY

You are not alone in your feelings of frustration and disappointments at work. Some people are more sensitive than others; however, all people experience upsets at work to varying degrees.

I can relate to you. At age 21, I felt a phenomenal deficit in my ability to communicate with others. I was shy and unsure of myself. In high school, my angst was so bad that I would be physically sick to my stomach before I attended any social event. I had severe anxiety and social phobia.

When I was finishing my undergraduate degree, my final requirement was to student teach at a junior high. I had already "college hopped" four times (in the days when education costs were still manageable), so I didn't want to change schools or majors again. However, the thought of standing in front of a roomful of teenagers made me want to not only switch my major, but leap to a fifth college – I was terrified to say the least. And my fears were compounded by my imminent meeting with the "prophesizing professor."

But I decided to bite the bullet.

My undergraduate university assigned a professor to confer with a prospective student teacher prior to student teaching to predict how well that student would perform. My lowest point came on the heels of a feedback session with this one professor. As I sat across from him, I felt his words pierce my heart.

"Susan, I don't think you'll do well student teaching, I don't think the kids will like you or identify with you, and you're going to fall on your face and fail."

What a pep talk, huh? I sat there in a catatonic-like state, wounded and feeling horrible.

Then I left the building without saying a word, sat on the campus lawn and cried.

But, this story has a good ending. What made that possible was a summer respite before returning to student teach in the fall, during which I did two things. First, I enrolled in a Dale Carnegie Human Relations and Speaking Course in Upstate New York. The rigorous, yet supportive class met once a week for four hours for fourteen weeks, and I had to speak in front of a full room of peers at least twice during each session.

Second, I scripted lesson plans and painstakingly practiced the material I created to an audience of stuffed animals. (By the way, they make for a great crowd . . . particularly with a laugh track.)

I returned to college with a renewed sense of self-confidence, ready to student teach, and taught my heart out. At the end of my student teaching assignment, I was offered an unprecedented full-time teaching position.

Criticism is inevitable and happens to every living person on the face of the earth. There are techniques you can use to deal constructively with criticism, which we'll cover a little later on. The important part about being criticized is to realize it can and will happen at any time. It's your reaction that makes a crucial difference between feeling defeated or feeling empowered.

The experience of student teaching was a milestone, a springboard, a launching pad. After I graduated from college, I thought work would be a kinder environment, civilized and sincere. As you well know, some of it is; however, in the business world, people make derogatory comments, say inexplicable words or do unethical deeds. When I first began working as a young professional and was met with rejection or criticism, my initial reaction was to feel frustrated and shot down. Oh yes, and helpless, hopeless and discouraged, as well. But you don't have to feel that way!

I tackled my frustrations and disappointments by learning more about the human psyche and myself. While working full-time, I pursued first a master's degree in communication studies and finished, seven years later, with a Ph.D. in Human Development. Besides a personal, cathartic experience, I discovered why some people say the things they do, how we can respond constructively and proactively to others, and how we can be resilient rather than succumb to defeat, anger or irreparable damage. Most important, I learned practical, concrete steps that you, too, can apply to any situation to help resolve the problem at hand or what's bothering you.

You can be assured, no matter where you work or go to school or chose to live, there will be people who will rub you the wrong way and who will make you react adversely. Take for granted that these people exist and you will occasionally find yourself facing them on the same path.

Although you will always be confronted with challenging people, you can use these practical skills to help both you and the other person - as well as your organization move forward. You don't have to feel like a victim. I discovered that through my own school of hard knocks and twenty years of applied work experience. Today, I own a company that helps people develop personal power in communication, leadership and interpersonal relationships.

In each chapter of this book, you'll read about typical challenges we face with one another at work and how to resolve them. Here's a quick look at what's ahead.

Chapter Two covers the age-old question of why people treat you the way they do.

Chapter Three shows you why the most important answer lies in how you treat yourself and how you can teach others to treat you.

Chapter Four will help you take the risks you need in order to change your life.

In Chapter Five, you'll get valuable communication basics that will save you and others time.

Chapters Six and Seven demonstrate how you can confront others in a positive manner and how to get what you want.

Chapter Eight covers questions about how to handle criticism from others and how to give constructive feedback.

Chapter Nine will answer another commonly asked question, "How Do I Gain Credibility and Respect From Others?"

Chapter Ten addresses how to be a better speaker and presenter in small meetings or before a large audience.

Finally, *in Chapter 11* we'll consider when to leave a situation, job or relationship. You'll ask yourself specific questions to help you make that decision.

At the end of each chapter is an activity that will help you think about your own situation, clarify difficulties you are having and work toward resolving them.

So let's get started!

Chapter Two

WHY DO PEOPLE TREAT ME THE WAY THEY DO?

*This is the story of the scorpion and the frog. A frog was peacefully lounging on a lily pad, doing what frogs do in a calm pond. A scorpion approached the frog and asked him, "Will you give me a ride on your back over to the other side of the pond?"

The frog replied, "Why would I do that? If I give you a ride to the other side of the pond, you will sting me with your tail, and I'll drown!"

The scorpion answered, "Why would I do that? That makes no sense because if I sting you, then I'll drown, too."

The frog pondered the scorpion's logic for a few seconds and thought to himself, yes, that makes sense. If he stings me, then we would both drown.

"O.K.," agreed the frog, as he paddled over to the pond's edge so the scorpion could get on his back.

When they had arrived almost to the middle of the pond, the scorpion quickly whipped his tail and stung the frog. As they were both beginning to drown, the frog asked frantically, "Why did you do THAT?!"

The scorpion simply stated, "Don't you know, it's in my nature?"
* Original Story by AE MAXWELL

Jerome Kagan, of Harvard University, has categorized four types of birth personalities which include *timid, bold, upbeat* and *melancholic*. Kagan claims that there are even different brain activities and patterns for each type. Accordingly, 15-20% of us are born timid, 40% of us are born bold, another 20% of us are born upbeat and 20% melancholic.

So you ask, why do people treat me the way they do? The primary reason is it's simply in their nature. They are predisposed, as Kagan would claim, and their brains are genetically wired. Therefore, they act in a certain way.

My neighbor, Tim, is timid by nature. In a cautious, quiet manner, he is always trying to do things for other people. He and his wife recently had a baby. He is attentive to both his wife and baby much more so than most people would probably perceive the average husband to be. It is a joy to watch the care and tenderness Tim takes when holding the baby or speaking with his wife. He will likely never be someone who is loud or gregarious.

Tim told me one day that he avoids confrontation with others. He works as a postal carrier with his own route, which allows him freedom and very little contact with people.

My colleague, Karla, is quite bold in the way she approaches life. She tends to be outspoken and assertive in her manner. If there is a problem in a store, she is confident in openly confronting the manager or person in charge to find a resolution.

When Karla and I were on a business trip in Kauai, one of the Hawaiian Islands, we had some time off and decided to go for a hike together. Kauai is a magical place. On the north end of the island is the lush, paradise-like Na Poli coast where mountains meet the ocean. The colors are vibrant greens and blues, and tropical plants and fruits grow everywhere.

On the other side of the island is Waimea Canyon, also known as the Grand Canyon of the Pacific because of its close resemblance. While it's not as large as Arizona's Grand Canyon, it is nevertheless spectacular. This is where we decided to hike.

After a three-hour hike up and down variegated terrain, we came upon the zenith overlooking the Pacific Ocean. It was breathtakingly beautiful. Karla spotted a small herd of mountain goats on adjacent cliffs about half a football field away. The only thing connecting us to those cliffs was a narrow ledge. It was a windy day, yet, Karla decided to venture out onto the ledge, which was probably ten feet wide with a 3000-foot drop.

As I watched her spring out onto the ledge, enthusiastically exclaiming she wanted to see the goats, I could feel my toes tingle. I, the chicken, stayed back on secure ground. All I could imagine was Karla plunging to the depths of the canyon. She faired just fine.

Karla's nature is bold, adventuresome, and bigger than life. She becomes energized from taking risks in unfamiliar territory. In her work, she is an entrepreneur and owns a business. She tends to take chances and confronts others with no hesitancy.

People with the upbeat birth personality seem to be good-natured and positive.

I have three brothers, one of whom is extraordinarily upbeat and good-natured. Steve is always looking for the good in situations. You could give him a box of dirt for his birthday, and he'd say, "Wow, this is a nice box!" My family moved a lot when my siblings and I were younger, and inevitably, within a few days, Steve would have four new friends in tow. Today, he is a successful salesman. People still gravitate toward him.

We all know people who have a pervasive sense of sadness or melancholy. They can't seem to find the silver lining in their lives. They are frequently sad and seem defeated when things go off track at work. They usually feel responsible and stuck without a solution.

The purpose of describing these four birth personalities is not to rate people or judge them. There is no one birth personality, which is good or bad or right or wrong. It's just each person's nature to be the way he or she is. But no matter what your dominant birth personality is or what someone else's birth personality is, keep in mind two points. First, it's important to become aware of your birth personality and be adept at reading other people's. Second, once you recognize the birth personalities, you can become skilled at interacting and problem solving with different personality types.

Let's imagine an office environment where all four of these birth personalities work. We can't know for sure which personality type would have which job, but we can hypothesize. For example, Karla, the bold birth personality is the office manager. She handles all the administrative duties and manages other support staff. Steve, the upbeat birth personality, is the salesperson for the company. Tim, the timid birth personality, is the company's financial analyst. The fourth birth personality, the melancholy one, Leslie, is the technology manager.

Let's say there is a problem with the office financial software that is affecting Tim's work. How do you think each person's birth personality will play out, given this scenario? Karla will most likely take the initiative and call Leslie to fix the problem. If Leslie can't correct the problem immediately, Karla may become bolder. Karla's aggressiveness may make Leslie feel melancholy and defeated. Tim will likely observe from a distance as the stronger personalities interact. Steve may serve as a buffer and help solve the glitch in an upbeat manner.

This scenario gives you a glimpse into how personalities play out in the workplace and offers one theory as to why people treat you the way they do. You can look at it as people on automatic pilot.

In addition to each person having a birth personality, we as children are exposed to a particular environment, which also influences our adult behavior.

Let's go back to my neighbor, Tim. He told me once that he is an only child and was raised by his mother. She has what you could define as a bold personality and made most of the decisions for Tim. If Tim is timid and his mother is bold, who do you think was more dominant at home? Right, Tim's mother. Tim also chose a style of relating to his mother as one of consideration. He tried to make her happy. Most likely, he wasn't going to stand up to her because he felt overpowered by her.

In the context of work, if Tim has a manager who is bold, he will likely take a secondary role. This does not mean Tim couldn't learn to be more assertive over time. In fact, with practice and effort, he can.

Tim could, instead, have been raised in a family where he was encouraged to speak up. What if, when he spoke, his mother said, "Tim, that's a good idea. I'd like to hear more." Imagine how different he might be today if that had been his childhood environment.

No one family environment is perfect. Parents make mistakes, and children make mistakes, too. Because environments range on a continuum from very supportive and nurturing to destructive and damaging, it is inevitable that our family environment will influence our behavior at work.

In addition to the nature and environmental explanations of why people treat you as they do, there is an abundance of research on how we behave as adults, given the role we played within our nuclear family. Our nuclear family includes brothers, sisters, and parents. Yours may have consisted of caretakers or a foster home. They, too, influence our behavior.

A client recently told me that she does not like to engage or interact with others, rather she prefers to keep to herself in her cubicle. In her family, as a child, she would make her parents and siblings guess what she was thinking. She liked the attention she received from her family when she behaved that way and to keep her family wondering what was going on inside her head.

She continues to play this role, and it has been a double-edge sword. She was recently promoted to manager of the creative department at a public relations company, and her preferred way of communicating is to make her staff figure out what she is thinking. Her non-expressive face and mannerisms offer no hint of her thoughts, either. As a result, she has had a conflict with several of her staff because they are unclear of her expectations. Her lack of clarity and directness has cost the company money on several occasions.

Another client of mine, Jaime, has three sisters and no brothers. His parents divorced when he was 10 years old. He had a timid personality at the time and a very bold and melancholic mother whose temperament fluctuated from day to day. His father left home, and his mother moved away with him and two of his sisters. Jaime's mother had an extremely hard time after the divorce, spent many days crying and couldn't function well. Jaime took on a caring role with his mother and sisters. He worked while in high school and gave his paycheck to his mother to assuage her moods.

Jamie became used to his role as someone who tried to make things better for his family.

In his job today as a school psychologist, he counsels young underprivileged kids and provides them with wisdom and insight. He learned his caring role early in life and feels comfortable with it.

I know of a CEO who is very effective, but he uses intimidation tactics with his staff. He will berate, belittle and scream at them.

They, in turn, believe the CEO thinks they are easily replaceable, particularly if they don't follow his orders. When the CEO was a young child, his father died, and he assumed a lot of responsibility. He had a couple of younger brothers, and so he became a tough decision maker for himself, his mother and his brothers. He learned early by being single-minded and rough, he could get what he wanted.

There is research to support the idea that you more or less assume a role at work, which is similar to that of your role in your nuclear family. In Amy Stark's book, *Because I Said So*, she claims that we consciously or unconsciously react to people around us at work who replicate our siblings or prominent people from earlier years in our lives. It follows, then, if you were criticized by perhaps your brother when you were young, and if you never knew how to respond to your brother other than by getting angry and running away, then, in theory, you are likely to respond the same way as an adult when a man criticizes you at work.

Or let's say you were the most talkative in your family as a child and you had free rein to express yourself constantly and, in fact, there were no boundaries set for you. You will probably display these same behaviors at work and may be viewed as a strong, challenging personality.

We are reinforced in our early roles, and that tends to encourage us to continue that behavior again and again, even as adults.

Finally, keep in mind that someone you're having difficulty with may have a learning disability such as attention deficit disorder, a chemical imbalance in their brain or a mental illness. Mental illnesses are varied, and statistics indicate 20% of the population—one in every five people—is experiencing some form of it. These include the more common types such as depression, anxiety and impulse control, and the less frequently occurring types such as bipolar disorder, borderline personality and schizophrenia. A person's mental health will certainly affect his or her behavior at work. Some people address these illnesses with therapy and medication. Unfortunately, studies show that the majority of people do not seek help.

Resist the temptation, however, to rush to the conclusion that the person with whom you're having a difficult time is mentally ill, therefore hopeless. And remember that your co-workers, like you, can be stressed from a myriad of home pressures, work issues and relationship troubles, all of which take their toll.

We could continue to theorize about the reasons why people treat you the way they do all day, but more important than the reasons is this:

No One Does Anything To You Deliberately. Let me restate that. *No One Does Anything To You Deliberately.* This includes people in the business world. Just as you handle things in your own way, which may be your nature, what you've learned at a young age through your environment, your role in your family, your mental health state, or how stressed you are, other people deal with things for the same variety of reasons.

Here's a practical example. You learn to do something at a young age, such as having temper tantrums. Then you see that people tend to give you what you want to shut you up. You then try it again, and again you see that your tactic works. You become used to that way of acting. Whether a help or hindrance to you, your behavior is one of a knee-jerk reaction, hard-wired by decades of use, otherwise known as a *habit of response.*

Someone else learns to be easily defeated, gives up quickly, blames others and gets attention for that behavior. That person has also formed a pattern of behavior otherwise known as a *habit of response.*

Why do people treat me the way they do? 13

Try this:

Write your name like you normally do in the margin of this page. Pretty easy, huh? Now put your pen in your opposite hand and write your name. Do you feel like you are four years old again? How we behave, or react, given a particular situation, is like writing with our dominant hand. We are used to responding in a way that is familiar. Again, that's why *No One Does Anything To You Deliberately*. And other people treat you the way they do because of their habits of response, like writing with their dominant hand.

I'm not excusing bad behavior. Many times, people's behaviors are pitiful, obnoxious, annoying and disgraceful. But until they are held accountable or asked to change, they may not realize the negative effects of their behavior on others.

A friend of mine from Boston once said to me, "People do what they do until they don't do it anymore."

The first time I heard that, it felt like a thunderbolt hit me in the head. The statement is profound in its simplicity. The idea is this: People treat you the way they do because it is who they are, all they know or learned at an early age. Their behaviors have become habitual. And you can bet they *will* continue to treat you that way until:

A) they become aware of their behavior and learn a new way to treat you and others,

or

B) you confront them and let them know that their behavior toward you is inappropriate, which results in their taking action to change their behavior.

The *Eureka* for you is understanding that *You have a choice when interacting with people at work. You are NOT a victim!*

This is so very important, because with a choice to change your reaction to others, you have power.

We can spend hours, days and years assigning a reason as to why people treat us as they do. Knowing the possible reasons is part of the puzzle, and that's why I spent time covering it.

But what is most important is your reaction. You cannot change another person's nature, former environment, family or mental health. You can *only* change the situation when you *change your reaction*. And you *can* change your reaction!

Applying This to You:

Your Nature, Environment and Family of Origin.

1) How would you classify your nature? Are you bold, timid, good-natured or melancholic? You may be a combination, and that's fine.

2) Describe your family of origin. With whom did you have your primary relationship(s)? Your mother?, father? sister? brother? grandparents? foster home?

3) In your family, what were the communication patterns? Who had the most "air" time? When and where did you express your thoughts?

4) How was conflict handled? How did you resolve problems? Who was the dominant person? Was it you?

5) What was your communication like with the dominant one in your family?

6) How resourceful was your family to goal set and solve situations?

7) What "role" did you play in your family as a child? Were you a high-risk taker? a care taker? a comedian? a loner? a bully? How were you reinforced for your role and feelings?

8) How did you react when you didn't get what you wanted as a child? Do you react similarly today at work? What are the common denominators of your behavior as a child and today?

Chapter Three

HOW YOU TREAT YOURSELF IS MOST IMPORTANT

Oprah Winfrey has said time and time again that we teach others how to treat us. That sounds so strange, doesn't it? But it's true! Our reactions to people give them permission to continue - or not continue - treating us in a particular way.

Most people's behavior is commonplace to them, because they, without a doubt, have been doing whatever they've been doing most of their lives. Think about that for a minute . . . haven't you been responding to situations and types of people in a particular way most of your life? Others are no different. But, you can change the way people treat you by being aware and making choices. Be aware of how others are treating you and be aware of how you chose to respond to them.

Think about this. You drive the same route to work everyday. One day, a colleague asks you where you live.

"I live right near you," she says. "What road do you take to get to work?"

You tell her. She replies, "You know, there is a faster route. There are back roads, but they'll cut seven minutes off your commute."

Now, two things are apparent. First, you have a new awareness about an alternate route to drive to work. Next, you have a choice. You can continue taking the same route to work, or you can drive the other route.

The same is true of our reaction to others. We have a "route" of reacting to people whom we find difficult. All of us have been conditioned and trained (remember our nature, environment or role in our families) to treat others and react to certain situations and people. This is called our *route of reaction*. Metaphorically, it is the most common road we drive to work.

When you clash with another person, it can feel like being in a bumper car - a lot of contention and discord. You may feel like you and the other person come from different planets because of the way you see things. This interaction can elicit feelings of injustice. You may wonder, how dare someone be so unreasonable, sarcastic, and rude. How dare they treat you that way?

Or, you may feel you can control others' behaviors by reacting in a certain way such as intimidation or throwing a temper tantrum so that you get what you want.

I'm here to tell you that you do have a choice. You can take another route to work. You can react to another person in a positive, more productive way. You can create new routes, and, by doing so, you will feel self-respect and self-empowerment.

How do you know if you need a new route of reaction? Well, if something feels uncomfortable or gnaws at you or makes you physically ill, those could be signs. If you constantly put up with something or feel infinitely frustrated, those, too, are indicators that you probably need a new route of reaction.

The key is that only you can do this for you. Only you can choose a new route of reaction. When someone treats you a certain way that you don't like and you don't say something to her, she most likely will repeat her behavior. You have to let her know that you find her behavior unacceptable to you.

After I graduated from college, my very first professional job was with a state agency in Albany, New York. I was an entry-level person, technically known as a research analyst, working among eight, bright, highly educated, senior analysts. None of the analysts were my immediate bosses, but I did various projects for all of them.

One of my first assignments was for an analyst named Steve. Steve handed me a typed paper with the names and various locations of 12 doctors. He said, "Susan, what I want you to do is call this list of doctors and invite them to a conference."

I was so eager with my first assignment. So I grabbed the paper and went back to my cubicle. Two days later, I emerged enthusiastically and found Steve.

"Steve, I called all the doctors and invited them to the conference," I said, smiling. He silently looked at me with an expression of disbelief. Then, while rattling the paper and pointing to the list of doctors, he yelled, "Why did you call these two doctors?!"

I thought it was a trick question and replied, "Because you asked me to?"

Steve retorted, "I didn't want these two doctors called. Now everything is ruined, and I'll never give you anything to do again as long as you are employed here."

Well, I felt as if an arrow had gone through my heart. I ran away, taking the elevator up to the observation tower on the 54th floor. Obviously I didn't jump, but I cried . . . a lot.

A very compassionate co-worker from the Bronx followed me to the observation tower twenty minutes later.

"Susan," she said. "Let me put this in perspective for you. First of all, no one was killed, and that's a good thing. Second, no large amount of money was lost, and that's a good thing, too. But, his ego was bruised, and maybe that's not such a good thing, but that's the way the working world works, so get used to it."

I thought to myself: get used to it? you have to be kidding! But, in retrospect, I can now see that I selected the same route of reaction as when I student taught. I fled the scene of conflict and went to the observation tower to cry. I did not solve the problem, and I didn't give myself much empowerment through my behavior or thoughts. I ignored all future interactions with Steve and said things to myself that weren't very helpful.

Perhaps you've had these same thoughts: "I'm a failure." "I'm going to be fired." "People aren't going to like me." "I'll never get another assignment." "I'll mess up future assignments." "I'm a loser."

I defined myself, at that moment, through my perception of Steve's evaluation of me.

But, Steve also took the wrong tack. It wasn't helpful to solve the issue at hand by screaming at me and telling me he'd never give me anything to do again. His route of reaction was excessive and unproductive.

The good news is that the incident didn't have to end like it did. In the following chapters, we'll revisit this scene among others where you'll learn how to confront others in a positive manner, how to set boundaries with people, how to engage in conversation with someone you see as difficult, and how to problem solve challenging situations.

Right now, think about these ideas as tools and resolutions to both prevent and solve difficult scenarios. Ask yourself, if this situation were to repeat, are there practical questions I could ask in the beginning to gain clarity. For example, regarding Steve, I could have repeated back the assignment to make sure I understood his directions. I could have checked in with him after the first few phone calls and given him an update on my progress.

Ask yourself if the anger you are feeling is really about the other person or some unresolved issue within you. For me, Steve represented an extremely critical person. I didn't deal well with criticism when I was younger. His telling me I was inept escalated into a huge insurmountable monster in my head. It's good to get in touch with your triggers and work to overcome them. There will always be your version of a "Steve." If you don't address what's eating you inside, it will repeat indefinitely, until you do.

Are you being reasonable when you don't speak with someone to resolve an issue? It may feel like you have the upper hand, but do you really? Ask yourself if it would be better to let go of the ill feelings. Are you cutting off your nose to spite your face?

It always amazes me how doors open when I take the initiative to approach someone with whom I've had a run-in and sincerely say, "You know, this just isn't working. Can we come up with a better way?" This, of course, is aside from any blatant physically or mentally abusive behavior. No one should endure that.

If someone is speaking to you in an unacceptable manner, you have every right to say, "I'm not willing to discuss things with you until you talk to me in a civil tone or without swearing." I could have said to Steve, "Obviously you are upset right now. I'll come back later to discuss this with you when we both are more level-headed."

There is a professional speaker who says that you can negotiate anything with someone who trusts you. How do we gain trust? Through consistently matching our words and actions, which benefit both you and the other person. Have your words and actions been mutually beneficial?

Keep in mind that we all are someone else's difficult person. Even if you are "nice," you may be perceived as not being assertive enough. Or if you are assertive, you may be seen as not warm enough, and on and on.

If you are wrong, admit it, apologize directly to the person and move on. This is an extremely powerful strategy. Remember, don't place yourself in the position of a scapegoat. At the same time, realize that others can't move on until they feel understood, and you get what they are telling you.

The *Eureka* for you - *It is always better to address an impasse or problem with another person early on.* Letting the situation ruminate to the point of irreparable damage is not good. It will only result in a worsened interaction. You can take the initiative to respond differently and change an outcome.

Applying This to You:

How You Treat Yourself and Teach Others to Treat You.

Think about how you treat yourself and others when in a difficult situation.

1) Describe your last challenge with someone at work. Who was it with? What happened? How did you respond to that person? What was your route of reaction?

2) What messages did you say to yourself? What was your behavior after the incident?

3) What different reaction could you have chosen which could result in a mutually beneficial outcome?

Chapter Four

YOU HAVE TO BE WILLING TO TAKE A RISK!

Think about an accomplishment. It doesn't matter when it happened in your life or what the accomplishment was. It could be finishing a project or raising a family or getting promoted or winning an athletic contest - anything. Do you have one in mind? Now think about what you did to achieve that accomplishment. Why were you successful? List three reasons.

1. _____

2. _____

3. _____

Did you say perseverance? focus? desire? tenacity? a plan? pursuing your goal in spite of obstacles? The same reasons you were successful in achieving your accomplishments will make you successful with your interpersonal goals at work. Dale Carnegie courses put forth a concept called "earning the right." What they mean by that is when you work very hard at something in life and you have experience to substantiate your efforts, you have earned the right to talk about it. Can you speak about the accomplishments you just listed and how you finally got there? Can you discuss how you set your goals, the steps you took, the cost to you, and the sacrifices you made? Sure you can! And no one can ever take that away from you.

When you work hard to achieve something and you increase your skill base, you build your confidence in you, which will manifest in your demeanor and actions: a confidence and strength of character, which is indisputable.

The same is true for interpersonal skills at work. You can set your goals and persevere. The payoff for you? A tremendous sense of liberation and freedom from having to respond in old, ineffective ways to a given person, persons, or set of circumstances. Doesn't that sound appealing? Think about your response to someone who gnaws at you, whom you talk about incessantly, who doesn't listen, with whom you just can't seem to connect? What if you could respond in a different way that made you feel empowered rather than merely stunted, victimized or hotheaded?

You can, but you have to be willing to take a risk and change your behavior. Only you can do that for you. I can't. Your mother can't. Your best friend can't. Your significant other can't. But you can! And that's the only way you would want it, too.

Several years back, a major university conducted a study to determine what makes people happy. Isn't that information alone worth the price of this book? What do you think? Some people said religion, but that would mean religion would have to be viewed by everyone in the same way, and that's not going to happen. Other people said a hobby or exercise; however, there is no one hobby or exercise for everyone. Researchers found that the key to happiness is first to know what you want and then be willing to take a RISK to get what you want.

Why don't people take a risk? Simple – they are fearful of what they have to give up.

Part of taking a risk is giving up something. It could be giving up a way you think about someone, or a job you don't like, or finances. And it takes time and effort and focus. However, you won't just give up something for no reward. There is the light at the end of the tunnel known as the payoff.

Recently, I spoke with a manager who said over the past three years his management ability has increased tenfold. I asked him why he thought that to be true. He said, "Well, I realized that being a jerk and dictatorial wasn't working anymore. People respond better to being treated like valued human beings."

Eureka! And it may seem like "duh" to you, but for him, the notion was life-altering. He had to give up the idea that he was on the throne as a manager and instead communicate with his staff as valued, thinking, feeling, productive people. He had to take a risk with no guarantee, but it has provided him with phenomenal results.

Think about what you want to change and what the risk would be for you. If you know the risk, and you want to move in a new direction, then you have to create a plan and do something differently. I mentioned earlier in the book that I was scared of people when I was younger to the extent of being physically ill when faced with new situations. You may feel similarly when you are faced with unfamiliar situations. Most people do. However, you're going to empower yourself with small steps and climb higher on your ladder of goals.

I can now speak in front of thousands of people. It's great to go from being so scared to speaking confidently in front of a crowd. But, I didn't magically transform from being afraid of people to speaking in front of large groups. That would be a great trick. Instead, I took small risks.

During my junior year of college, a boyfriend, who was aware of my self-consciousness and fear of others, said to me, "Susan, just say anything when you're with a group of people. Don't worry about it being the best thing to say. Just say anything."

I took his advice. I recall a time when I was with a group of friends and acquaintances, and I said, "It's a nice day today."

The people in the group just said something like "Yeah, it is," and smiled. I thought to myself, OK, it's a start. Sometimes it's as simple as that. I also had to give up the security of never trying. I had to give up my not having a voice. Taking a risk in tiny amounts can pay significant dividends.

My oldest brother, David, took a risk around his 40th birthday. David is the principal trombonist for the New York Metropolitan Opera Orchestra, "the Met," in New York City. Indeed, this prestigious orchestra is one of the world's best. From elementary school through high school, David practiced extremely hard, often six hours a day.

He went to the Julliard School in New York City on a scholarship and won a position with the Met, through competitive audition, at age 21.

Well, as you can imagine, David was feeling somewhat burned out 20 years later. The Met, as with many professional orchestras, is demanding, and David worked on major holidays and often played grueling back-to-back four-hour operas.

Around the time he turned 40, he felt he needed a break. He took a sabbatical and enrolled in film school at New York University. Yes, film school! He took a risk to enhance his professional resume. Remember, he had been playing the trombone since he was eight years old.

David wrote a short script for a 30-minute film, which took him over a year to write. A part in the script called for an elderly man. David ventured and sent his script to Hume Cronyn, who lived in New York City at the time with his wife, Jessica Tandy.

New York City has about nine million residents, so the chances of running into anyone in particular on a given night is comparable to winning the lottery. However, to my brother's amazement, his ticket came up. Two days after sending Hume Cronyn his script, David was dining at a restaurant and saw Cronyn also dining and reading his script. The next day, the actor called him at home, said he liked the script and agreed to be in the film.

David also had a cattle call for an actress to play a small part of a nurse. One hundred women auditioned, and he selected a little known actress at the time . . . Calista Flockhart.

After his film was finished, "Angel Passing" was accepted by the Sundance Film Festival, as well as many others, and has won 14 awards.

This inspiring story is not about films or orchestras or Hollywood or celebrities. It is about being willing to take a risk. My brother knew about playing the trombone in orchestras. This was the set of skills he had built and reinforced and perfected throughout the years. He didn't know anything about producing and directing films, except that he had a vision and was willing to take a risk.

He also worked in small steps. He enrolled in film school to get a flavor for the field. Then he spent a year writing the script. He had to hire the actors, handle his finances, get permission for filming, edit the film, etc. This all took time and effort, but the payoff was worth it.

Here's what will happen for you, too. You will take small, incremental steps, and soon those steps will accumulate into significant skill development for you, until one day you'll look back and realize how much progress you have made. And you'll be the same age regardless of whether or not you took the risk!

And here's the *Eureka*: *If you don't work toward your happiness goal, it takes just as much time and effort to stay with something that makes you unhappy, as it does to take a risk and work toward your happiness goal.*

Of course, the path is never linear. Sometimes you may feel you take three steps forward and one back. Right before David was finishing his film, he had to have the negative frames of the film glued by a negative cutter. The negative cutter mistakenly cut into a sequence of frames, destroying one of the most crucial shots of the picture. That mistake cost my brother $12,000 to correct.

So there will be ups and downs, but if you persevere, you will reach your goal. Don't be lured into thinking that you can circumvent your way to strengthening your skills and changing your direction. Don't be deceived into thinking that famous people, our peers, or managers achieve things overnight. They don't.

Early in her life, Britney Spears began learning stage presence and performing as a mouseketeer in the Mickey Mouse Club. Ricky Martin began acting in a soap opera while singing locally in his native Puerto Rico. Oprah Winfrey started as a news reporter in Tennessee. Diane Sawyer was a weathergirl. Comedian Bob Newhart was an accountant. The stories are infinite. What these people had in common was a goal, training and perseverance. They had the same abilities to accomplish their goals that you do!

Here's how you get started. State specifically what you want to achieve or change. The more specific you are, the more likely you will reach your goal. For example, you can begin with a general goal such as, "I want to be a better communicator." Then break down your goal into steps.

My brother had a general goal to expand his professional resume. Then he listed specific steps. He'd apply to film school, complete the application, register for specific classes, study scriptwriting, learn about camera angles, etc. When he accomplished these, he decided on his next goal, which was to write a well-crafted script and then write the script chapters by a certain date.

The same concept applies for your career goals and communication goals at work. In addition to being a better communicator, include specifics such as improving your problem-solving ability with your boss, controlling your anger, or speaking at meetings with more confidence. Those goals are specific and measurable and will enable you to design an action plan for yourself and chart your progress.

It's also important to break down your goals into manageable tasks. When I was finishing my doctorate, I had the harrowing job of writing the dissertation. I employed the swiss cheese approach. That approach allows you to break down your goal into manageable tasks. I wrote everyday, sometimes for only 15 minutes or a half hour, but I made sure I wrote everyday. You'd be surprised how time adds up. After a few months, I had most of my dissertation written. This method was much more achievable than if I thought about the 180-200 page document I had to research and write.

Carol Shields, who wrote <u>Stone Diaries,</u> was interviewed on NPR not too long ago. She has five children. The interviewer asked her how on earth she found the time to write while raising her children. Shields explained that every night she would take out a yellow legal pad and write for two hours before she went to bed. She said she was disciplined about writing every night. She finished her first novel in six months.

To review, the first step is to establish a goal and write an action plan with manageable tasks to achieve your goal. This approach will serve you well. Don't worry about the time it takes you to achieve your goal. It is an incremental process. Most people worry so much about the goal itself or what other people think of their goal that they never get started. Before they know it, a year goes by, then two, then five, and they still haven't started toward their goal.

My friend, Pete, is now in his early forties. He is a successful salesman; however, he never finished college. He asked me 20 years ago if he should finish college, and I said yes. Then 10 years ago he asked me if he should finish college, and I said yes. I think it's fine if people do not attend college; many people have been successful without a college degree. But Pete has always wanted to sell pharmaceuticals, and in that field a college degree is a must. Recently, he was almost hired for a pharmaceutical sales position, but he didn't get the job because he did not have a college degree. If Pete had started 20 years ago, even 10 years ago, he could have a degree by now. If you break down your goal and take each task at a time, you will see results.

It's also important to work on one goal at a time. Don't be overly zealous and spread yourself too thin. You may over commit and get discouraged. Instead, set incremental tasks; you'll build more confidence and feel motivated by seeing yourself complete each goal in sequence.

Applying This to You:

What Do You Want? What Are You Willing To Risk?

1) What is your communication goal at work? Be specific. What would you like to achieve? Write your overall goal. Maybe it is managing anger, perhaps being a better speaker, or reworking an old relationship with a colleague.

2) When you purchased this book, what answer were you looking for? What problem did you want to solve? That's a good place to start.

3) If you could wave a wand and change something, what would it be?

4) What risk(s) do you need to take? What do you have to give up to gain?

5) Next, write specific, measurable steps. You can think of them as tasks. Try writing the tasks on sticky notes and arranging them in chronological order. That way, after you achieve each task, you can remove the note. And remember, sometimes you may take two steps forward and one back.

List each specific task and your time for finishing the tasks.

You can create these measurable steps for anything you choose. If you want to eliminate your reaction of anger at work, the first task could be to investigate an anger management class in your community. The next tasks could be to enroll in the class, attend the class and take notes, then practice in a given situation using the steps the instructor offered.

If your goal is to repair a relationship with a colleague, the first task might be to make a commitment to repair the relationship with the colleague. The second task could be to define your intention or desired outcome with this person. Perhaps the next step would be to call this person and set up a meeting. That's how it works. Even taking the smallest, simplest initial steps will help build momentum and move you in your goal direction.

You can do absolutely anything you set your mind and heart to do. People do it all the time. The difference between those who achieve their goals and those who don't is that the people who do have a plan never, ever give up.

Chapter Five

FOUR STEPS TO BRIDGE THE COMMUNICATION GAP

There are basic principles for effective communication. Imagine yourself on one side of a gorge and the person with whom you are communicating on the other. There is no bridge to connect you. You communicate by yelling at one another. You think you are communicating, but, oops, two days later, the other person does something differently than what you thought she would do. You think to yourself, "Wait a minute. We talked about that ... better yet, we yelled about it. What happened?" The more you skip the basics, the more apt you are to fall into the gorge. You widen the communication gap, which can lead to misinterpretation.

Sometimes the stakes are quite high. Experts now advise you to mark your body prior to surgery to indicate what part the surgeon should cut so you don't have the wrong limb amputated or procedure performed! Even hospitals are susceptible to communication breakdowns between you and the person with whom you are communicating. It may feel strange or uncomfortable at first (like writing with your opposite hand), but the payoff for you will be immense. When you build the communication bridge, you dramatically decrease your potential for error. In addition you increase your ability to create a positive outcome, including a meeting of the minds, shared understanding, focused problem solving, enhanced learning, and tangible results.

Let's spend some time reviewing these communication basics.

From the following example, try to surmise the first basic communication principle. There's a brief demonstration that I use in training classes where I tell the audience that I have a dog, which is true. Then I say to the audience, "I want you to see me walking my dog down the street," as I walk across the room or the stage with my arm extended, pretending I'm walking my dog. Then I ask the audience, "What kind of dog do I have?" Sometimes I'll have someone point blank say, "How do I know what kind of dog you have?" I tell them to guess. Most people will answer enthusiastically and say, "I think you have a Golden Retriever, a Rotweiller, a Poodle." One time someone yelled, "I think you have a live dog." Right, live dog, that's good. Good start. I'm not a taxidermist. After about four (usually incorrect) responses, I tell the group I have an Airedale Terrier and that she looks like me – long limbs and two-tone hair. They laugh, and then I make my point. Do you know what it is?

An enormous Eureka for you: Don't assume anything!!

Read this again: *Don't assume anything!!*

Most of the time, when you make an assumption, you will be wrong. Studies show you will be wrong 80% of the time. This happens to us everyday in our communication. We assume we know what someone is talking about when, in actuality, we don't. Or we think another person understood our meaning, and they didn't. That's why I like to use the very simple dog example to illustrate this point. The audience thinks they know what kind of dog I walk, which they usually don't. I act as if I'm being clear on what kind of dog I'm walking which, of course, I'm not.

Why does this happen? The first reason is that we all have a different frame of reference. For example, if I said to imagine a home, what do you see? a house? townhouse? with a lawn/without a lawn? with a fence or no fence? who's inside? you and a family? you alone? Maybe you don't see a physical structure. Maybe you get a feeling which is not describable.

Maybe you get a negative feeling. No two people would answer exactly the same. That's because you have a unique frame of reference based on your knowledge and experience.

Similarly, if you asked a group of people why they chose to work where they work, do you think they would all say the same thing? No, they wouldn't. They also wouldn't necessarily give the same answer as you. Some people would say they chose where they work because it's close to home; some would say for the money; some would say because of their friends at work. Some would say for their job responsibilities. Some, because they make a difference. You shouldn't assume other people would make the same claim. When we assume that we know what someone is talking about (through our own lens), we risk misinterpretation.

Listening is very difficult. Did you know that you can think much faster than someone can speak? That leaves quite a bit of space in your head if you're the one listening. Invariably, people will listen to you and then drift away and listen some more and then drift away. You do it, too. We all do. And, if you just plain don't like what the person is talking about, or don't like the person herself, that, too, will make it difficult to concentrate on listening.

You'll probably use that extra time in your head to carry on an internal dialogue that sounds like, "What is that outfit he's wearing? ... that's dated ..." Or, "I have no idea what she is talking about, but I'm going to stand here and act like I do. I hope she'll hurry up so I can say what I'm going to say." Sometimes you get caught if someone stops talking, looks at you, and asks, "So what do you think?" Then you have to backtrack and ask them to summarize or repeat it. That can be awkward, especially if you don't know the person well, or it's your supervisor.

Distractions around you can make it difficult to listen. You can also have internal distractions. For instance, if you're upset emotionally because you just lost your job or are in the midst of a break-up, that makes it difficult to listen. Listening is challenging, but it's critical to listen and not make assumptions in the communication process. That's the first basic communication principle.

The second basic communication principle is: *Paraphrase and ask clarifying questions.* Paraphrasing is the act of repeating back what you thought the other person said. For example, if you said, "My commute here today was terrible. There was a traffic accident that made me an hour late for my morning meeting. My boss was mad at me, and it's only Monday!" I could then respond to you, "Seems like you got off on the wrong track today between your long commute and your boss's disapproval." I just paraphrased what you said. This is different than offering an opinion on what you said. I'm simply checking in to make sure I understood what you said. Paraphrasing also works well to eliminate false assumptions that you may have made when you were listening. Paraphrasing validates the other person's words and makes the person feel important. Don't underestimate the power of paraphrasing.

When you ask clarifying questions, you gain further information about what the person said to you. For example, I have a colleague, Wanda, who is a talented, diplomatic professional. Wanda is paid on commission, however, she hasn't been paid for several months. Now, as you well know, unless you are independently wealthy or have huge savings, that makes for a difficult way to live.

Wanda approached the owner of the company, where she works, to inquire about payment. The owner responded, "Sure, you'll be paid soon, when other business contracts are signed."

You see how Wanda literally can't afford to make assumptions at this point? From the reaction of the owner, what words jumped out at you? Was it, "when other contracts are signed?" Wanda needs to get clarification on that statement. Wanda can simply ask, "What does that mean? I'd like to know specifically how many contracts? What is the time frame? After the contract is signed, how soon can I expect to be paid?"

If Wanda doesn't ask, then the situation will continue. When you respond as Wanda did through asking questions, you are being fair and straightforward. And you are asking for the same in return.

Here's another example. Let's say that you are working with a peer on a project, and he says, "I'll complete the part I'm good at." Again, what does that mean? Do you know what part, for sure? No, you don't, and you don't want to make an assumption. You need to ask what he means by that? He could respond, "You know, my creative ability." Then you can say, "Please be specific. Are you saying the concept, the writing, or the design?"

Be assertive in your communication. In our enthusiasm for a particular outcome, we sometimes avoid doing the work up front. Do not take for granted that you know what someone is talking about. The types of clarifying questions typically include what, when, where, how, and why. If you do not know the answers to these questions, you take a huge risk by not pursuing the answers. Do not simply hope that you know or think that you know, and don't ignore what you know, just because you don't want to take the time and effort to find out or you are worried about what the other person(s) will think of you.

The third principle is: *How you say something is absolutely critical*! I once had a woman in a seminar who stood up and said she had a question. As she proceeded to pound her right fist into her left hand, she said, "I'm clear on what I expect of my staff, but I can't understand why they don't do what I want them to do!" Then she sat back down. There were about 200 women in the room, and, after she returned to her seat you could hear a pin drop. It was soooo quiet. I said to her, "Would you like some feedback?"

She replied, "Sure!"

I walked over to where she was sitting and started raising my voice while pounding my fist into my hand. Then I asked her how she felt about my communication. She said in a quieter tone, "That feels intrusive."

A number of years ago, there was a landmark communication study conducted at UCLA. Albert Mehrabian studied the elements of communication that had the greatest impact on us. For instance, when someone is speaking to you one-on-one or in a meeting or in front of a large group (NOT over the phone or e-mail), what has the greatest impact on you, the listener? Your choices are words, voice tone and body language. Body language includes your eye contact, gestures, facial expressions, posture, dress and cologne/perfume. Words are your actual words spoken. Tone evokes an emotion such as excitement, worry, or complacency.

Think about the question and how you would respond. Divide words, voice tone and body language in percentages (first, second and third) as to which impacts you, the listener. They must add to 100%. For example, you could say 20% for words, 50% for voice tone and 30% for body language.

Words _____

Tone _____

Body Language _____

100%

Four steps to bridge the communication gap

Dr. Mehrabian determined that body language is first with 55% impact on us, voice tone is second with 38% impact and words are third with 7% impact. That means voice tone and body language account for 93% of someone's message. Words only account for 7%. Are you surprised?

If you're skeptical of the numbers, know that there is a lot of data to support this claim. UCLA researchers didn't just ask one person down the street and say, "Yo, you ... you look pretty smart. What would you say?" They asked thousands and thousands of people.

Think about it. Doesn't it make sense? See yourself sitting among an audience of 500. The speaker is introduced. She comes out slowly and shuffles her notes. She then sits in a chair, leans to one side, her arm on the armrest, and looks down. She begins speaking in a monotone voice and says, "I'm Missy White, and I'm here to talk to you about raising sales in your company." She then looks at her nails while continuing to speak. You might be thinking to yourself that your pager's going off soon, and you're going to have to leave the room and make a call, wouldn't you? How disinterested would Missy appear?

Imagine, you are in a room of 100 people. What if your company president had to make a serious announcement that he had to layoff 35% of you, due to low earnings for the year? He sprints into the room, very upbeat and, while smiling, says, "Geez, I'm sorry to tell you this, but we have to have layoffs this year." He looks down and chuckles while continuing, "You know, we're just down on our profits. Sorry." That would be ludicrous!

Or pretend you begin a new job. You attend your first meeting, and the staff is sitting around a table. Your boss' boss appears, arms crossed and with a military-like, stern tone and posture, and says, "Welcome to the meeting. We're going to rearrange our department into teams. I want you to feel comfortable participating. OK, who has the first thing to say?"

In all three examples, the person's words don't match his/her tone or body language, and when that happens, we tend to believe the person's tone and body language.

You might be wondering about the importance of words in academic and technical circles. Well, let's see what that looks like. Let's say you were at a business meeting, and you met someone you did not know, and he says to you, in a condescending and patronizing tone, "Well, while I was at Harvard, we believed that . . ." Then he continued to speak to you in an arrogant tone all the time pointing at you. What typically happens is that you become distracted. You can't truly hear his words because his tone and body language are so offensive to you. This is why the voice tone and body language account for 93% of our communication.

In academics where everyone knows information is presented in a didactic style, words account for 11-12%. A slight bit higher, but again, tone and body language impact us the most.

To emphasize the point, have you noticed when people around you are speaking a foreign language that you do not know, you can almost understand what they are saying? Through their tone and body language, you can tell if they are happy, upset, concerned, etc.

A major reason that you can interpret their message is because there are six universal facial expressions, mostly conveyed through eye movements. They include happiness, fear, disgust, surprise, anger, and sadness. These emotions have been studied as far back as Darwin. Sometimes there is a slight variation in the list with some researchers adding shame, anguish and rage.

Have you been wondering what happens over the phone? What do you think the percentages are for words and voice tone? Voice tone accounts for 90%, words 10%. If you want to test this, listen the next time your partner tells you he/she loves you over the phone. (In a non-chalant tone) "Love you a lot, hon. ... I'm gonna stop by Wal-Mart and get the batteries and light bulbs." That's good news and bad news, right? The good news is that you heard the words, "I love you," but it didn't quite have the same zest as in 1982, as his/her tone conveyed otherwise.

We also lose about 15% of our voice energy through the phone lines. If you can, tape record yourself while speaking over the phone. (You don't have to tape the other person, just yourself.) Most likely, you'll find that your voice sounds flat, and you'll want to increase your enthusiasm when you're on the phone.

A final note on words, tone and body language in the context of e-mail. Be careful with sending messages via e-mail that are emotionally laden because you open yourself up to significant misinterpretation. Ideally, e-mail should be used for facts, dates, data and other objective information. It's advisable *not* to give negative feedback or emotionally evoking information by way of e-mail, because you lose 93% (tone and body language) of your message. And if you want to give someone feedback that is unfavorable or favorable, give them the courtesy of, minimally, a phone call and, ideally, an in-person visit. You will garner respect that way, strengthen your rapport and control hard feelings.

Nothing can replace face-to-face communication for building trust. The phone comes in second place and e-mail, third. Even teleconferencing doesn't replace face-to-face communication because you miss the interpersonal group dynamics of real time communication.

What are the implications for you? Just as you are paying attention to other people's 93% of communication through tone and body language, other people are paying attention to yours. Ask someone you love and respect to give you feedback on how you come across when interacting with others. Are you expressive? hard to read? upbeat? serious? Do you gesture? smile? How is your posture?

It's important that you are open to receiving feedback. Keep in mind that you are merely gathering information to improve your communication skills with others. That's why you want to ask someone who respects you and not just anyone. This will help enormously by raising your awareness.

A few years back, a couple of people told me that I needed to improve my posture. I respected their opinion and tried very hard to be aware of my posture. Wow, did it help! I look more confident, assured and professional. I was very grateful to my friends for telling me, because these qualities are so important. As a side benefit, my breathing improved because I was standing up straighter, and as a result I had more energy and projected my voice better.

You may want to ask several people for feedback. Ask them what they perceive are your strong communication points and those you should develop. Then listen for common themes in what they are telling you. That will give you a sense of balance with their perceptions.

Being aware of your strengths and areas to augment is the first step. The next step is *practicing* new skills. The more you practice, the better you will be. When you communicate well, people will think it comes naturally to you, and that's OK. Don't mind if they think that way. You don't have to tell them how hard you've practiced. Just simply smile and say thank you and congratulate yourself on your progress.

The last communication principle is: *Create a shared sense of meaning that leads to a result.* How many times have you walked away from someone thinking that you both understood one another, only to be disappointed a few days or weeks later? This most likely occurred because:

    a)   you made an assumption that was incorrect,

b) you did not ask clarifying questions, or

c) you didn't clarify what action would be taken.

This might sound like a lot of work, and you're right, it does take effort. *However*, if you take the time to communicate optimally:

a) you will create a mutually desired result,

b) it gets easier after time because you're building your skills,

c) you'll set a precedent of how you will communicate in subsequent interactions with others, and

d) you'll feel empowered.

You may also be wondering, why you always have to be the one to facilitate the communication process. Consider that the other person has less awareness or is less capable than you. Be proactive. This will give you a sense of control in your communication interaction and a better chance of getting what you want.

Let's go back to Wanda. To recap, she has not been paid in several months. As we realized, she needed to have a discussion with the owner of the company. Wanda said, "I've worked very hard this year and would like to get paid for the work that I've done."

The owner said, "Our agreement was that you would generate sales of business contracts of X amount and then be paid."

Wanda responded, "Yes, and I've brought in Y amount of business contracts year to date. The other amount I will bring in by year's end. Are you willing to pay me commission for the income I've generated so far this year?"

The owner said, "Yes, I can pay you only for the work you've done so far."

At this point, Wanda *does not* want to just end the conversation and walk away. Wanda needs to paraphrase.

She may say something like, "I heard you say that you are willing to pay me for the work I've done so far to date, is that correct?"

Now keep in mind Wanda's tone and body language. Her body language should be respectful, professional and direct. Wanda should maintain eye contact with the owner. There is no need for Wanda to be belligerent, sarcastic or disrespectful.

After she hears an affirmative response from the owner, Wanda also needs to ask, "OK, we just agreed that I will be paid for the work I completed to date. When can I expect (with respectful tone and body language) to be paid?"

The owner replies, "You'll be paid soon."

That's not a specific enough answer. Wanda can then say, "When is soon? I need a time frame."

The owner says, "Friday."

Wanda can even press further and say, "When on Friday?" The owner may respond, "Friday at noon."

Two critical things have now happened. Both parties are clear on what will happen in the near future. Can you see how they created shared meaning instead of simply making assumptions or general remarks? They also know what specific action will be taken. Wanda will be paid Friday at noon.

You *can* avoid assumptions and avert misunderstandings by listening, paraphrasing and asking clarifying questions in a professional manner. Your challenge is to create mutual respect and understanding, which will result in shared meaning and follow-through action steps. If you don't do this, then you end up where you started and continue to feel helpless, frustrated and angry.

You can use this method for all your communication interactions with people. Always review the final solution and action(s) with the person. Make sure you repeat what each person needs to do before you conclude your communication.

Let's look at the situation where you're working jointly on a project with the colleague who says, "I'm going to work on what I'm good at."

You can then ask, "What part is that?"

He responds, "Proofreading."

You say, "OK, so you're going to proofread and edit what I write, is that correct?" He says yes, and then you can clarify, in a non-threatening tone, by saying, "OK, I'll write the text and then give it to you to proofread and edit." This way you clarify what each of your roles will be on the project.

In my experience as a trainer and organizational coach, I have found that most miscommunication is really no communication at all or poor communication. Even the communication basics we discussed take time and energy, but again, the time you spend up front will pay off. *Eureka!*

To review of the four principles:

1) *Do not make assumptions.* Never assume you know what the person is thinking or feeling.

2) *Ask clarifying questions* to lower your margin of communication error.

Next, remember that *voice tone* and *body language* account for *93%* of your message.

Words account for *7%*. Therefore,

3) *How you say something is absolutely critical!*

And finally, principle number four is:

4) *Create a shared sense of meaning* by making sure each person understands each other and his/her responsibility and what his/her next action is.

Applying This to You:

You and the Four Basic Communication Principles.

1) Think of the last time you made a wrong assumption. What were the circumstances? Who were the people involved? How did you make an assumption?

2) Considering the situation you described above, what can you do differently next time? What clarifying questions can you ask? Write out those questions here:

3) Ask three people about your words, tone and body language. Chart below who the person is and what they said. What did they say you do effectively? Areas to develop? Are there any patterns or repeated comments?

Four steps to bridge the communication gap

COMMENTS

PERSON   *WORDS*   *TONE*   *BODY LANGUAGE*

Person # 1

Person # 2

Person # 3

Is there something you'd like to change or modify? What risk will you have to make to give up the undesired behavior? What commitment will you make to work on your tone, body language and words?

4) Think of someone at work with whom you have no clear future action steps. What aspects seem vague? What can you do to engage him in conversation and create shared meaning? List those steps below as tasks. Check each one as you complete the task.

Chapter Six

CONFRONTATION IS NOT A FOUR LETTER WORD

Think back to the situation of Steve and me from Chapter Three. He screamed at me, and I fled to the roof. Neither of us attempted to solve the problem. Typically, this is what happens: Conflict occurs between two people, and, instead of engaging or conversing with someone to solve the problem, we tend to polarize from the other person.

The North Pole and South Pole are at different ends of the earth. Similarly, we become like opposite poles when we are in conflict with someone. We avoid having a conversation with him, and, often, we begin to recruit others to our cause. Does that sound familiar?

Isn't it typical to circumvent the person with whom we have the problem and complain to someone else? Here's how it might fall out. I begin to talk about Steve behind his back. I say to my friends, "That Steve, he's such a jerk. He asked me to call a list of doctors, and I did, and he yelled at me!" Of course, I'm going to get agreement for my case. My friends are going to say, "Oh, that's horrible. That Steve is a jerk!"

Meanwhile, Steve is doing the same thing. He's commiserating with his comrades and telling them, "That Susan, she's so incompetent. I asked her to call a list of doctors, and she called them!"

This approach is called *making the other person wrong*. We spend all our time and energy making the other person wrong and ourselves right. This can play out even further when we begin to make the other person's life unpleasant by, perhaps, gossiping about him behind his back, making up stories about him, withholding information or providing misinformation. We're so tempted to make the other person suffer and *get him to tell us how wrong he was and how right we are.*

Now, to take a tact like that may *feel* good, but it's not going to *solve the problem* and most likely will make circumstances much worse. When this happens, both parties lose sight of what the original issue was.

I'm not saying don't have feelings. You can have feelings and reactions *internally* in the best way you know how or talk to a trusted confidante. The best way I knew was to cry. The best way Steve knew was to scream. It would have been better if we had both initially reacted our "best ways" in private. Then we could reconvene to converse and figure out how to *solve the problem and discuss a solution.*

The most important loss for you if you merely *react* and don't solve the problem is you will not build your interpersonal skills. You will probably get reinforcement from others for being right, from your perspective, but you will also limit your communication expertise. This is an important point to understand. If I can only cry when something unfavorable or challenging occurs to me, then I am handicapped in my ability to solve the problem every time it happens. Likewise, if Steve can only scream at people every time something he doesn't like happens to him, he is limited. Instead, you want to be able to develop several ways to respond and deal with the issue(s) and people at hand. That will give you a greater sense of self-empowerment. You, ultimately, won't feel as frustrated, angry or distraught.

In order to feel more self-empowered, you have to give up making the other person wrong! Rather, think more about how you are going to solve the problem and try different communication strategies with that person.

I know many people who have confronted others in a damaging way, and it has had devastating effects on their jobs, even careers. Throughout this chapter, I'll impress upon you to think first and react second. Use the minimal three-hour rule. After a conflict, don't do anything for at least three hours. Walk away and compose yourself before you say something that you can never take back. I've heard from a number of stellar professionals that it's not what happens to you that matters, but how you react to the situation. A professional is cool, composed, and confident. The 3-C formula for the 3 hour rule!

Before you confront another person, I want you to ask yourself some questions:

1) *What is the purpose of confronting this person?* Go back and review the mishap in your mind.

2) *Is the dilemma solely his fault?* Did you perhaps have some responsibility in what happened? With Steve, I take responsibility for not clarifying the assignment up front.

    In addition, I didn't subsequently solve the problem or alleviate the tension between us. True, he was in a higher position in the department, but no matter your place in the organizational chart, you have to be proactive and always thinking. People often ask, how can I influence upward? One way is by being proactive in your communication.

3) *Can you improve the situation by applying communication tools?*

4) *Can you forgive what happened and put it behind you?*

5) *Will this dispute matter one year from now, five years from now?*

Unnecessary conflict occurs all too often in work settings. There is a sense of righteousness from others that once someone goofs, there's no resolution. Is it worth it? I see people swearing at each other in meetings, yelling, crying, shutting down. How many times have you put someone in his or her place or alienated him or blown up? Was it beneficial? Did it move you and the other person forward? Were those actions constructive in the long run? What are the risks of confronting someone with the purpose of telling him off?

There are four reasons why people don't do what they're supposed to do.

1) They may not have the *knowledge*. For example, if I asked you to recite the alphabet in Russian, and you can't, it's not your fault certainly . . . you don't have the knowledge.

2) They may not have the *ability*. You may have knowledge of golf but you don't have the ability to play the game.

3) They may receive *mixed messages, conflicting or confusing assignments or lack the resources* to complete the assignment. You can't paint a room without paint and a paintbrush.

4) They just *don't want to* or *won't do* the task or job.

This last reason on the list is often the place managers and co-workers erroneously jump to first. Did the person you are about to confront have all the necessary resources they needed? Is she knowledgeable, able and competent? Was the goal clearly communicated? Were there checkpoints built in for dialogue and discussion?

Before you confront someone, it is a good idea to think and gather data first.

In the case where someone is abusive to you, you would respond differently. In Chapter Nine, I clarify the difference between abusive and inappropriate behaviors versus annoying and challenging office behaviors.

Right now, I want you to focus on garden variety work occurrences that lead to confrontation. For example, perhaps someone gave you the wrong information, or she didn't follow through on an assignment. Maybe a co-worker gossiped or lied to you, a peer took credit for your work, or you were overlooked for a salary increase, etc. How do you confront people from situations such as these in an effective manner?

Confrontation is not a four letter word. <u>Webster's Dictionary's</u> second definition of confrontation is a "face to face" meeting. American Sign Language has a confrontation sign meaning a person-to-person meeting. This is the same approach I suggest you use.

At this point, a face-to-face meeting may sound extremely awkward and intimidating. You are going to feel like you're writing with your opposite hand. Remember, though, the purpose is to mutually solve an undesirable situation. *Using this strategy you make the problem the issue to address rather than attacking the individual.* This way, you both walk away feeling better, and you solve the problem.

Forming an alliance with the other person to find a solution to the problem should make things feel less threatening to you. Again, in order to do this effectively, you're going to have to give up making the other person wrong and rubbing his face in it. Instead, concentrate on coming to a resolution.

The basic six steps to facilitating a confrontation are:

1) *examine your purpose,*

2) *express a common goal,*

3) *uncover each person's contribution versus blame,*

4) *outline the facts,*

5) *propose solutions, and*

6) *agree on the next step.*

The first step is the most important. Ask yourself this question. At the end of my confrontation, an ideal outcome would be (fill in the blank)_____. Your answer may be to make sure you and your co-worker figure out how to have 100% phone coverage or to be able to check each other's work grammatically or to meet once a week to discuss office issues. Using this purpose, you focus on the problem to be solved and not the person.

If your answer is to make him see how right you are and how wrong he is, then you're not ready for a face-to-face meeting. When was the last time you were motivated by, "You SOB ... you stink! You are wrong, I'm right, and you'll change right now!" See the point?

In the second step, express a common goal. State what is mutually beneficial and of interest to both of you. This is where you make the other person your ally. If there is no benefit to her, why would she invest time to solve the problem?

In the third step, *listen* and talk. Explain the problem as you experienced it and have the other person do the same. Until you both have the opportunity to explain how you see things, you can't move forward. Step three will also allow you to diffuse the emotional stuff. This step is extremely important. Keep in mind that the other person will want to be heard and understood. Until she feels you get it, she won't move on. This is a basic human principle. Remember, too, if you did make a mistake, apologize and direct the conversation toward problem solving. Admitting to someone that you made a mistake or agreeing with what someone is saying is a powerful diffuser.

In the fourth step, outline the facts, as you know them. Now you have moved away from addressing feelings and stories to stating the concrete, observable facts. These will include dates, times, people involved. Facts are not conjecture.

In the fifth step, both parties propose solutions to resolve the problem.

During the sixth step, you agree on the next measure to take. This may include beginning an action or collecting your thoughts and deciding to meet at a later time.

Once again, let's look at the scenario between Steve and me, using the six-step confrontation model.

"Steve, I'd like to discuss what happened the other day, so it doesn't happen again."

Steve replies, "Well, I'm really upset by that whole thing. You really messed things up." I say, "I think we were both frustrated with what happened. Let's straighten it out so it doesn't occur again. I have a of couple ideas that may work, and I'd like to get your input."

What did you observe by this transaction? You probably saw a few things. First, I didn't pull any punches. I came right out with the purpose of why I wanted to speak with Steve, which was, "I'd like to meet with you to discuss what happened and problem solve a solution."

Confrontation is not a four letter word

Now I could have said, "Steve, I'm here to tell you that you are the absolute worst person who ever existed." And you know what, that may have felt good but it won't help me solve the problem or build my skills. And I will make an eternal enemy out of Steve.

The other step I took was to create a common alliance between Steve and me to solve the problem. I moved toward a solution. I didn't say, "Well, you idiot ... if you had been clearer with the assignment, we wouldn't be in this mess." I took the high road. I made him an ally, rather than an adversary.

You also probably noticed when Steve said, "I'm really upset by that whole thing, and you really messed things up," that I did not say, "Oh yeah, well you're the loser ... "

However, I also *didn't* say, "You know what, you're right, I'm sorry. I did mess things up, and I'm just no good. Can you ever forgive me?"

Instead, I acknowledged that we both were responsible. I acknowledged that we both contributed in some manner, rather than blaming him. How was I responsible? Remember, never make assumptions. Ask clarifying questions and paraphrase, as we reviewed in Chapter Five. I should have repeated back the assignment to Steve when he first delegated it. That would have been helpful. Something like, "O.K., I understand you want me to call the doctors on the list and invite them to the November 5th conference. Is that correct?" Steve would simply say, "Yes," or "No, I just want you to call doctors one through ten on the list." It's especially important to paraphrase after someone has given you an assignment or any piece of information that includes an action on your part.

It's good to develop a habit of repeating what people said. Steve could have been distracted, upset, or just not thinking when he gave me the assignment. I could have been preoccupied or misunderstood him, also. Be proactive rather than reactive.

Watch your tone, too. Always be professional, confident, and sincere. I've had people say to me, " I'm not going to be professional because they're not professional." The problem with that argument is you have made them your role model on how to behave, by duplicating their poor behavior. You are repeating the very thing you despise.

The next step is to outline the facts. Facts are not emotional. They are things. They are objective, concrete and measurable. I was given a list of doctors' names to call. That's a fact. Steve would also say he gave me a list of doctors. We would agree on those facts. This step is important, because you're now moving the individual toward agreement with you. Facts are very difficult to dispute. Once the facts are established, you can address a solution.

Possible solutions would be that I could review the assignment with Steve. He could ask me to say what I thought I heard, after he gives me my next assignment. We could also check in with each other a day after the assignment is given to make sure everything is on track. We would then agree that we change the process the next time Steve gave me an assignment.

Make sure you verbalize your agreement. This will sound like, "OK, Steve, next time you give me an assignment, I'll repeat it back to make sure we both understand one another, and then we'll touch base the following day." This way you bring the discussion to closure, and you're both clear on subsequent actions.

If your discussion was complicated or you still feel unsure, you can always follow through with an e-mail or memo. You could write, " In agreement with our discussion on May 15, 200__, we'll follow a new procedure which is_____. Thank you for your efforts to make our team more productive."

Let's apply the six-step confrontation model to another example. A woman presented me with a dilemma. Renee told me she had worked for a healthcare company for one year. During her first year of employment, she was enrolled in management classes sponsored by the company. It was her understanding that she was to be placed in a management position after successfully completing the classes. Yet, when she spoke to the department manager, after completing the classes, he told her that she would not be promoted yet. I asked her if he gave a reason, and she said he indicated that it wasn't going to happen.

Here is a confrontation opportunity. It's advisable that Renee have a face-to-face meeting with the department manager whom we'll call Frank. After Renee examines her purpose, she will schedule her meeting with Frank. Her purpose is to understand why she is not in line for the management position and how to make it happen. Renee would say to herself, "At the end of my discussion with Frank, I want to know why I am not in line for the management position and what I need to do to make it happen." It's important for her to keep this in mind before and during the time she meets with Frank.

When she meets with Frank, she will state the common goal. Something like, "Frank, I'd like to revisit why I'm not moving into the management position we discussed last year. We have both invested time and money in this endeavor. I'd like to understand why it's not happening now and what we need to do to make it happen."

At this point, Renee has covered two of the six confrontation steps: her purpose for the discussion and their common goal of time and investment in the management training.

The next step is to talk about contribution rather than blame. Renee could say something like, "Frank, when I was hired last year, we talked about the opportunity for me to take management classes for the purpose of acquiring a management position, and yet now you say no. I'd like to understand how things got off track."

It's difficult to know how someone will respond, but let's say Frank says, "Renee, now is not a good time for promotions. Ben just left the department, and we're short-handed." Keep in mind Renee's original purpose. She does not want to talk about staff hiring or Ben. She doesn't want to be sidetracked. Her purpose is to understand why she's not moving to a management position and how she can make that happen.

When you reach an impasse with someone, stay on your purpose and ask clarifying questions. It's temping to say, "Frank, you pulled a bait and switch. I spent 12 months working my butt off, and now you say it's not going to happen. Watch your back. I know where you live and the car you drive."   Don't do it!

Rather, say, "Are we starting this discussion from the same assumptions? We agreed in October of last year that I would begin the management program in November. Our agreement was if I successfully completed the program, I would be in line for a management position the following December. It's now December 28. I have passed the course, but am still in the same non-management position. If you understood things differently, I'd like to hear."

Frank responds, "I know, Renee, but things have changed since then. The timing is not good now."

Renee should get Frank to recommit and be more specific. She wants to get Frank to move forward. She could say, "Frank, I understand your reason why I'm not being promoted now because we're short-staffed. We both agree we had the conversation last year about my promotion contingent on completing the classes. What has to happen at this point before I'm promoted? How do we close the gap?"
Frank says, "After we hire Ben's replacement, we'll talk."

Renee should now paraphrase, "O.K., Frank. After Ben is replaced, we'll talk about my management position." Renee could add, "I'd like to get involved in the hiring process. We learned interviewing skills in the management classes. Could I sit in on the candidates' second round of interviews? This would help both of us. I'll get practice and exposure, and you'll get a second opinion of potential candidate competencies and department chemistry."

It wouldn't be unreasonable for Renee to follow through with an e-mail, reiterating her conversation with Frank about their discussion and next steps to get her to a management position. Did you notice how Renee moved in a positive, constructive mode toward problem solving? She didn't blame Frank or argue with him or punish him. She outlined the facts of their prior discussions by using dates and goals. They arrived at a solution. She used the word "we" often to make the problem solving a joint venture. Renee even offered to help with the interviewing process. She included the benefit for Frank.

Renee's tone was professional and straightforward. She wasn't sarcastic, bitter, solemn, or belligerent. Where people often get into trouble is they don't address a situation early on. They wait until it festers and becomes so enormous that they can only erupt or explode or deal with it emotionally. Or they refuse to speak with the person altogether, sometimes for years at a time!

When you take the higher ground and apply the six steps, you'll encourage respect for yourself and from others. Not everyone may like what you say, but if you do the right thing, which is mutually beneficial, he will think more of you. Do things underhandedly, and he'll think less.

The *Eureka* for you is *when you have trust with another person, anything is negotiable.* How do you gain trust? *By synchronizing your purpose, words and actions.*

Notice that you're not being a pushover, either. You are taking a stand and resolving the issue. When you find yourself stuck during a confrontation, here are some more strategies:

1) *Sometimes a time-out is in order.* Perhaps you or the other person is too volatile. If that's the case, walk away and reconvene at a later time. However, don't go beyond 10 days to two weeks.

If you feel you are getting off track, review the six steps. Have you left anything out of the sequence? Make sure you are moving toward the facts and not participating in the blame game.

2) *Validate how other people see the situation as real and right to them.* This will work wonders in diffusing other people. Yet it does not mean you are agreeing with them. Think of the scenario of Steve and me when he said, "I'm really upset by this. You messed up and everything is ruined!" I could legitimize his remark by saying, "I can see you are upset and very concerned." Again, I haven't agreed with him, just validated what he said.

Another *Eureka* ... *people can't move forward until they feel they've been heard and understood.*

What about when you're not sure what the person is thinking? Maybe he is not offering information or doesn't know what to say. You could say:

"What do we know for certain?" or

"What do we think is true but we have no data to prove?" or

"What don't we know?"

Again, if things seem way off base with your mutually exclusive perceptions of the situation, you could say:

> *"Are we starting from the same or different assumptions?"* or
>
> *"What is your understanding of the issue or problem?"*

If you are unclear on next steps, you could say:

> *"What do we need to do to close this gap?"* or
>
> *"What has to happen for us to move on?"* or
>
> *"Ideally, what would you prefer to have happen?"* or
>
> *"What do you need from me at this point? What would make things all right?"*

If you need more information from the person you could ask:

> *"What ideas do you have about ...?"* or
>
> *"What do you understand the facts to be?"*

If you are speaking with your manager or you sense resistance from the person or you feel the other person doesn't have many suggestions, you could offer options, such as:

> *"Have you considered this?"* or
>
> *"What if you tried it this way for a month?"* or
>
> *"What if we try this on a trial basis? We'll talk again in three weeks."*

When you use these phrases, you're asking people to do something differently, without having to commit long-term.

When you have worked through the impasse, you want to propose solutions and agree on the next steps.

Like any skill, confronting someone takes practice. There also exists a paradox. Most people are afraid to confront another person for fear of the repercussions. *The irony is that when you confront others in a respectful, methodical manner, you gain respect, often solve the problem and establish or regain an ally. You also add to your repertoire of communication tools.*

Applying This To You:

Confronting Another Person.

Part One

1) Select someone whom you need to confront. At this point, do not select your nemesis! You want to build your confrontation skills and confidence. Chose someone easier. You can pick a co-worker, peer, supervisor, someone from a different department.

2) Sketch out the six steps, thinking of the situation and this person.

3) Role-play with a trusted confidante. Have that person give you some realistic resistance. Practice a few times. Does it get better with a few rehearsals?

4) Confront the person. Do not be hard on yourself (or the person.) Take notes afterward. What worked, what didn't work? What was your outcome?

Part Two

1) Chose another person whom you want to confront. Go through the six steps carefully. Remember, if you cannot see logic and only feel emotion, you are not ready to confront the person.

2) Again, write out what you will say.

3) Work with your confidante and role-play. Have your confidante be difficult. Try the line, "I'm sure I've contributed," when he tries to blame you. Agree on the facts. Admit when you were wrong. Practice moving toward a resolution and repeat the resolution before parting. Rehearse several times. How do you feel?

Remember: Have the courage to confront someone with the purpose of mutual gain. You *will* feel better and more productive!

Chapter Seven

HOW DO I GET WHAT I WANT?

What do you want from others that you aren't getting? Why aren't you getting it? Do you recall the biblical quote, "Ask and you shall receive?" I'm going to add a slight variation, respectfully, and say, "If you don't at least ask, you are assured you won't receive." "A person once asked me, "How do I get my staff to complete their paperwork?" I queried her if she knew why. She said, "I asked them a couple of times but stopped, because I didn't want to hurt their feelings or have them not like me."

Perhaps you can identify with these concerns:

> "I don't know how she will respond to me if I speak with her (it's been three years.)"
>
> "My boss will yell at me if I ask a question."
>
> "I don't know why my employee won't do what I ask."
>
> "I don't know how to get this person out of my physical space."
>
> "I don't like the language he uses around me."
>
> "What does she think of my work?"

Now typically, I'll follow up with this question. "Have you told her what you want?" The common response is, "No." I'm being quite sincere when I say that if you haven't asked someone

How do I get what I want?

for what you want or told her what you want, how would she know? It's helpful to clarify with the other person what actions you need to take in order to get what you want, move yourself forward, close the issue or come to a resolution.

A question listed on the previous page was, "I don't know how she will respond to me if I speak with her (it's been three years.)" The first thing I would want to know is: Why do you want to speak to her? What is your intention? Is it to mend the relationship? Then I would suggest you say just that. Something like, "I'd like to speak with you sometime about what happened with our friendship/relationship. I'm sorry things got so off track. I'd like to get things back on track if you're interested. I'll do what I can to make amends. I hope you'll consider what I just said." She may say she's not interested, but at least you tried. If she does say no, you can place your energy elsewhere. If she is interested, you're on the road to getting what you want.

A woman at a seminar said to me, "I see this man on occasion, and I really want to build a home with him, but he's inconsistent and only visits me once a month." When asked how long this has been going on, she said two years. Then I asked if she had questioned him about what he wanted and also told him what she wanted from the relationship. She said she was afraid to ask because she thought she knew the answer: that she was only a convenience and temporary person for him.

What if he did tell her she was a convenience or a casual relationship? If she thinks he would tell her that, then she needs to make a decision. If he is not what she wants and is only interested in a casual relationship, then it might be best if she moves on to someone who does want to build a home with her. Or, *she may have to lower her expectation.* Before she can make that decision, she needs to talk with him. She'll never know until they discuss it.

A *Eureka* for you: *You are the only one who can speak up for you.* You won't always get what you want, but at least you'll know what other people are thinking. You'll learn what needs to happen in order for you to get what you want. If the answer is no, you can move on and expend your energy in other places.

Unfortunately, in the workplace, people won't be vigilantly looking after you. It would be nice if they did, but they won't. Why? Because, just like you, they are thinking about what *they* want. Therefore you are your best advocate. It's wise to develop a voice and use your words favorably.

What about the statement, "I don't know what they think of my work?" Here are some suggestions:

1) *"When you have a minute, I'd like to talk to you. I value your opinion."*

2) *"I'd like to get your general thoughts on what you think of my work, both strengths and areas to improve. And if you could give me specific examples, that would be helpful."*

You might be thinking you can't just go up and ask someone that! Why not? If you don't, no one else will! And think of it this way: if someone said that to you, how would you respond? You'd probably think, OK, when do you want me to tell you about my opinion you value so much? Wouldn't you? Isn't that flattering?

Besides asking directly for what you want, it's important to consider your intention. What is your *intent*? If you want to prove to the person how wrong they are after three years, that, of course, will not bode well with anyone. However, if your intention is to share information and improve a working relationship, and you communicate that, you open a door which was formerly closed or which you never tried to open.

When you ask for something, consider that there are always at least two parties involved and both are thinking about themselves. There is a radio station that we all listen to 24 hours a day. Can you guess which radio station it is? It's not NPR or KISS FM. It's WIIFM or *What's In It For Me.* Think about it... what have you been thinking about for the past few minutes? Probably something like, how does this information apply to me? How can I use this information I'm reading? I'll read for 15 more minutes then I'm going to get something to eat. It's natural to think about ourselves and how we can benefit from a situation. This is also known as the **law of relevancy. If it affects me, it's relevant to me.** Knowing this, you have to take for granted that other people are doing the same thing. William James, noted psychologist, said that people think of themselves 95% of the time.

Children are egocentric. That means they think the world revolves around them and what they want. They see something and go after it. Adults are egocentric, too. Like children, they tend to see things from their perspective. The problem is, if there are two or more people involved, each one sees things from their own perspective. The critical point to consider when you want something from another person is *what is that person's perspective?* What does he *want?* What is he *thinking?* What is *relevant* to him? But we usually don't do that. Instead, we tend to try to convince people from our own perspective, which is a mistake for several reasons.

If the person you are trying to persuade has an emotional investment, he may have a hard time understanding your point of view. I know a realtor who gets very frustrated with prospective home buyers ... particularly first time home buyers ... because he feels they don't listen to him. John thinks that his clients should follow his suggestions without question. The only problem is his clients are not only investing a significant amount of money, but also choosing a home, which is a stressful experience.

John is successful and busy. He's dogged in his stamina and

leaves few stones unturned. He also has a direct manner and tone when dealing with people, particularly when he feels rushed.

Debra, a prospective homebuyer, called John and asked to be shown twelve houses that were one hour away. John suggested to Debra, in a direct manner, that she take the real estate listings and drive around the neighborhoods first to get a sense of which homes and neighborhoods would interest her, a prescreening of sorts. John thought that this way Debra would have time to decide what she liked while John helped other home buyers with impending sales. Debra called John's broker and said she wanted to work with another agent because John was too busy for her.

Interestingly, John and Debra had compatible outcomes or desired results. John wanted to sell a home, and Debra wanted to buy a home. However, if you look at the process, you can see a breakdown which led to the derailment. We know that Debra wanted personal attention and a warmer tone. John wanted to consolidate his time and help Debra when she was ready to focus on a particular housing area.

If we were to play back the interaction, John could have said to Debra in a non-rushed tone, "Debra, I know how important it is for you to receive personalized attention and focus (the WIIFM for Debra.) So that I can help you get that service you deserve, why don't you scope out some houses to see which are most suitable to you. When you narrow them down to a few, I'd be happy to show them to you (the WIIFM for John.)" As we discussed in Chapter Five, tone is so crucial, especially over the phone.

Here's another example. A client of mine likes to be called Elizabeth, her proper name. Since names are highly personal, we should all be called what we want to be called. Recently, Elizabeth was introduced to a new co-worker, who upon meeting her said, "Nice to meet you, Liz." Elizabeth retorted, "My name is Elizabeth," followed by silence. A few days later, Elizabeth learned that Jennifer thought she was snooty and stuck up.

How do I get what I want?

The important lesson to apply when we want something from someone is to consider each person's perspective. Elizabeth wants to be called Elizabeth (WIIFM for Elizabeth), and Jennifer wants to feel welcomed into her new job (WIIFM for Jennifer.) Neither Elizabeth nor Jennifer got what she wanted because each was seeing the situation from only her perspective.

How could they have approached the situation differently? Elizabeth could have *politely* said to Jennifer, "Please call me Elizabeth. Some people do call me Liz or Beth but I prefer Elizabeth. There's no way you could have known that, unless you read minds, so I'd thought I'd let you know." Jennifer would most likely respond in a congenial, accommodating manner.

It's so important to let people know what you want, find out what they want and negotiate from that point. You can't expect people to just know.

"How do I let someone know that they are in my physical space?" is a common question, particularly from women. In American business and conversations with unfamiliar persons, most people require a distance of at least three feet. In fact, I test this on occasion in my seminars and presentations. I'll have a participant stand in front of the room, opposite me, about 30 feet away. As I walk slowly toward him, I then ask him to tell me when to stop. Inevitably, he says, "Stop" at a distance of about three feet.

When I ask the group what they can do to have someone get out of their space, they'll say, "I'll back up." The problem with that solution is it's indirect, and the other person may not understand you. If he moves forward toward you, and you continue moving back, you've now engaged yourself in a dance that will end when you reach the wall!

Keep in mind that the best type of humor is about ourselves, and it's highly effective in interpersonal situations. If someone is in your space, you could say something like, "I'm going to ask you to step back a little. I come from one of those families where we need at least three feet." or "I need to see who I'm speaking to ... would you mind stepping back a little."

If you don't ask, who will? Asking does entail taking a risk, but expressed in a non-threatening tone, most people will appreciate your honesty.

Ascertain what the other person wants or their WIIFM. If you speak in terms of what she wants, too, she will be more apt to listen to you. Avoid using the statements: "You should do this." "I want you to do that." "You must think this way about that." If you talk to people in this manner, you will only repel them further. You don't like to be spoken to like that, do you? If you don't know what someone else wants, you can ask questions, in a calm tone, such as:

> "What is most important for you right now?"
>
> "What are you thinking?"
>
> "If you could describe your desired result or outcome, what would it be?"
>
> "What are your top three priorities?"

After you've uncovered what the other person wants, listen to her closely, and then repeat the information she just gave you. This will sound something like, "So what you'd like to see happen is ... " "In order for this to be a successful outcome, this has to happen, right?"

When you clarify someone's "wants," two things happen. First, you diffuse the situation by validating her, and second, she has provided you with more information which will serve to your advantage as a negotiating tool.

How do I get what I want?

Once she's told you what she wants and you've repeated her wants back to her, you can introduce your wants or WIIFM in a non-threatening tone and manner. Try something like, "I'm going to suggest that you also think about ... "

> "In addition, would you be willing to consider _____, for these reasons."

> "I understand what you're saying. Can we try it this way for two weeks?"

When you suggest your wants in that way, you make it less risky and threatening for her.

If you feel you've reached an impasse with the other person, refer to Chapter Six on "Confrontation is Not A Four Letter Word." That chapter offers questions you can apply to get further information and solve the problem.

One of the ways to move from an impasse that we talked about in Chapter Six is to find out what someone wants or needs and not just her position on an issue. Consider this: two people are sitting in a library. It is early fall, and there's a chill in the air. One patron stands up and closes the window. The other patron sitting nearby stands up and opens the window. The opening and closing of the window continues between the two patrons for a few minutes. The librarian notices the skirmish, walks over to the two patrons and asks what the problem is. One person says, "I am cold, and the draft from the open window is uncomfortable." The second person responds, "It's stuffy in here, and I want some fresh air." After listening to each patron, the librarian walks over to an adjacent window and opens it. Each patron is now satisfied. If the librarian had just considered each person's position of opening and closing the window, she couldn't have solved the problem.

If the patrons in the library tried to find out what the other person wanted, the problem would have been solved before the librarian intervened. One person could have said to the other person, "You obviously don't want the window up. What is bothering you or making you feel uncomfortable? Let's solve this problem together." In order to do this, you have to be willing to let go of making the other person wrong and solve the problem instead.

Applying This to You:

What Do You Want?

1) List something that you want in a given situation.

2) With whom do you need to speak with to get what you want?

3) Have you spoken to him before? What was the result?

4) What are the person's WIIFM/issues or concerns?

5) Script a conversation with him that includes his WIIFM's and concerns.

6) Write possible obstacles that you may meet in your discussions. How will you address those?

7) Keep a journal of your results. You'll be amazed at the outcome!

Chapter Eight

HOW DO I HANDLE CRITICISM? HOW DO I GIVE OTHERS FEEDBACK WITHOUT HURTING THEIR FEELINGS?

Let's tackle the criticism question. Think about why criticism is so difficult for many people, and why you think criticism is so difficult for you. Is it that you hate judgment? Do you dislike being evaluated? Do you feel criticism defines who you are? Does it feel like a form of rejection? Being candid will help you identify how you can handle criticism from others.

How does criticism make you feel? angry? sad? frustrated? powerless? It's important to be aware of what you say to yourself when you are criticized. Your thoughts become messages you tell yourself after you've been given unfavorable or constructive feedback. Those messages affect the way you feel about the situation, as well as yourself.

Take a moment to complete a brief exercise. Consider these questions and write down your answers. Think of a recent time when you were criticized.

What happened?

Who criticized you?

What were the circumstances?

What did you feel?

Why did you feel that way?

Think of another time you were criticized and ask yourself the same questions.

What happened?

Who criticized you?

What were the circumstances?

How did you feel?

Why did you feel that way?

It may be helpful to you to create a grid to observe your responses. Look for patterns in both scenarios. Do you notice any similarities?

Remember my stories about the prophesizing professor and about Steve at the government office who yelled at me? In both places, I reacted similarly. After the event occurred, I said to myself that I was no good, a failure, that I wasn't going to graduate or get any more assignments, or worse, get fired. My thoughts were illogical, although they created my feelings, so they were certainly valid to me. Likewise, your thoughts and feelings are valid to you. Yet, there are ways to respond to criticism that will help you feel empowered, rather than feeling victimized and reactive.

This may sound strange, but the first step toward productively managing criticism is to actively invite positive and negative feedback. What? Invite negative feedback? Am I crazy? No, and when you actively invite negative feedback, you cut people off at the pass. You begin to have a sense of control, therefore, you feel empowered in the interaction.

For example, in regard to the prophesizing professor, I could have said, "I'd like to hear some comments from you on how you see me in a positive light and then some things you would suggest I work on." In a work situation, you could ask someone, "I'd like to know how I help you now in your job and how I could help you further."

This method can successfully mitigate a tense situation when you are sincere. Can you imagine what you would do if someone at work sincerely asked you how they could help you do your job better? Wouldn't that take you back and feel disarming? In order to do this, you have to give up being right and move toward problem solving, making the other person an ally rather than an adversary.

The next step is to listen to what the other person says and understand what he means. When you react without getting all the information, you give up your power because you are reacting on an emotional level to what you presume the person is saying. Don't make assumptions. Instead, listen to understand what the other person is saying. Gather the facts and respond appropriately. Try not to take things personally.

Remember, listening is not agreeing. Suppose you say to me, "All people from New York City are rude." Now I'm from New York, and I want to understand what you mean, so I need to ask clarifying questions. I could say to you, in a neutral tone, "Why do you think all people from New York City are rude?"

You might respond, "Because I was in New York City one time, and I was totally lost, and I couldn't get anyone to help me. I asked two people for directions, and neither were willing to help me."

Again, I would clarify your response by paraphrasing and saying something like, "You think all people from New York City are rude because you asked two people for directions, and no one would help you?"

If you said, yes, I could follow with more clarifying questions.

This gives me a sense of control because I am gathering data. Be a good investigator before you react. Ask questions such as who, what, where, how, why, and when. You can then follow up with more questions or repeat what the person told you. It's important to summarize to make sure you understood what the person said and what she meant.

I could feasibly follow with, "How many people do you think are in New York City?" (said in a non-threatening tone.) There are approximately nine million people in New York City. I could follow with, "Do you think out of all the people in New York City there would be someone who would be willing to help you?" A question like that helps put the situation in perspective. *It also makes the other person accountable for her comments.*

After you gather all the information, you can acknowledge her by saying "thank you" or simply rephrase what she told you. If she still said to me, after my clarifying questions, "Everyone from New York City is rude." I could respond, "All right, I see you think everyone from New York City is rude, and there's no changing your mind." Another effective response is, "I'll consider what you said." Spoken in a direct, sincere tone with eye contact is quite productive. Even if I am from New York, her comments don't have to *annoy* me.

The last step is to go through an evaluation process. Consider:

1) Who is giving you the criticism?

2) How important is that person to you? What is the nature of your relationship?

3) Is this an isolated comment, or have you heard it before?

4) What will you do with the information you receive?

Your boss is probably a significant person in your life, as well as a close peer or co-worker. Someone standing at a bus stop or in a grocery store line is going to be much less important because she has less impact on your life. If you attempt to address every single remark that anyone makes to you, you will lose your marbles! Focus wisely on addressing comments from significant people on significant issues.

You also want to consider how many people have given you similar feedback. I'm about 5' 8" tall. I reached that height in junior high and tended to make myself shorter by rounding my shoulders, so I would be shorter than the boys. Well, that posture is not helpful in my role as a professional speaker, and several times people would suggest that I stand straighter with my shoulders back. It was a hard habit to break because I had perpetuated that pose for so many decades. Then one day, I saw myself on videotape, and I could clearly see what they were telling me. In my case, it did help me enormously in my professional image to improve my posture.

Sometimes the criticism isn't about you. It's about the other person, or what the other person is projecting on to you. For example, my colleague, Cindy, has been speaking for 20 years and always receives high evaluations from her audiences. One time a woman approached her after a seminar and said, "I want to give you some feedback. First of all, you remind me of my third grade teacher, and second, you look like a poodle." Can you imagine someone saying that? The woman giving Cindy the feedback was around 50 years old. Do you think the comments were really about Cindy, or could they have been about the woman giving her feedback? Perhaps the woman has some baggage from her youth? And what about telling someone she looks like a poodle? Cindy is very attractive and looks like she shops on Fifth Avenue in New York. Her good looks and style may have threatened the other woman.

In this case, Cindy had no relationship with the woman, and these were isolated comments. However, let's say that Cindy did care about the woman's comments. For example, we'll pretend she was an evaluator for the company that hired Cindy, and that her job was to give all speakers feedback and to determine if they would receive future work.

Speaking in a neutral tone, Cindy could say something like, "Are you the evaluator who was assigned to critique me?" "OK, you just told me that I reminded you of your third grade teacher. Describe your third grade teacher. How does that comparison relate to *this* evaluation?" All Cindy's questions should be asked in a professional, non-sarcastic, non-defensive tone. Cindy needs to be confident at this point. She is getting clarification, particularly since she's never met the evaluator's third grade teacher.

Asking questions makes the other person accountable and places you in a position of control and self-regard. The worse thing for Cindy to do is to react, because if she reacts, without learning more, she gives up her power to the other person. At the same time, Cindy intentionally or unintentionally becomes like her perceived adversary. Keep in mind that when you don't react adversely, you are not being a doormat. Rather, you will exhibit composure and control of the situation. Try it and see if you don't agree.

Cindy could also ask her in an inquisitive, professional tone, "You said that I look like a poodle. What does that have to do with the evaluation process, and what does that mean? Do you compare all speakers to dogs?"

Finally, Cindy will summarize. Let's say the evaluator told Cindy that she had a condescending tone and treated the group like children. "All right, you said your third grade teacher had a condescending tone? When did you think I used a condescending tone? Give me an example when I used an inappropriate tone."

The *Eureka* for you: *The person who is criticizing you should be able to tell you how she sees you now, what she thinks you are doing wrong **from her perspective**, and what she wants you to do differently.* This is called gathering evidence or data. If she can't paint you that picture, then her comments are unsubstantiated. One possible reason she can't give you an example is she may be trying to make herself feel better by putting you down. But she can't succeed at that without your consent. In addition, how can you begin to decide what action you're going to take if her comments are unclear?

In summary, when you receive criticism, each situation is unique depending on the individual giving you feedback. However, if you choose to respond by asking specific questions, clarifying and using an evaluation process, rather than by reacting, you will feel empowered and yield a better outcome for both parties.

How do you give someone else feedback without alienating him or hurting his feelings? Since you know what it's like to be on the receiving end of criticism, you can be empathetic when giving others feedback.

Before you give someone feedback, ask yourself, *what is your exact intention? Why do you want to give the other person feedback?* You have to be honest with yourself when you answer that question. *What do you honestly want the other person to do?* If you want to teach him a lesson, punish him, get even, or make him wrong, I'd think twice about giving feedback. It may feel good initially to even the score with him, but if you do, you likely will burn a bridge, and none of us can afford to burn bridges. Think about a time you did "let someone have it" and made a scathing comment. Were you still glad you said what you did six months later? What about if you ran into him at the grocery store? Would you duck for cover? Even feel a little sheepish?

I want to include a brief note here about unacceptable behavior. If someone makes abusive or inappropriate remarks, and you ask him to stop, and he continues, it's best if you report that behavior to your human resources department, to your manager or the other person's manager. For example, if someone continuously asks you out and you're not interested; if someone says something like "Hey, baby, I'd like to see you in the buff sometime." or "You are a dumb,@#$%^&, idiotic loser." You can respond by saying, "That is simply unacceptable behavior. Stop it now, or I'll take further action."

Inappropriate behavior aside, let's assume you're dealing with someone who isn't carrying his weight around the workplace, someone who doesn't seem accountable, or someone who continuously makes mistakes or misses deadlines. In these situations, ask yourself what your intention is before you speak with him.

The second step is to make sure you *time the feedback*. If it is March, you don't want to give him feedback for something he did last November. Usually, speaking to someone within a two-week window is best. Although each scenario is different, it's often not a good idea to speak with someone immediately after a mishap or blow-up, especially if a cooling off period is in order. Use your intuition and judgment.

Make sure that you speak with the person in a private area where others can't hear your conversation. If you can meet behind closed doors, that is certainly better than in a cubicle. You could also take the person to lunch, but make sure the tables are far enough apart from other diners so you'll have privacy.

When you are arranging a meeting time and date, tell the other person that you'd like to speak with him for a specified length of time. You can even tell him what the nature of the discussion will be. Try something like, "Bill, I'd like to spend about an hour with you to problem solve our missed deadlines." or "I'd like to speak with you about how we can better serve each other in our respective work roles." Whatever you say to the other person should be in line with your intention or purpose. If you say, "Bill, I want to speak with you about how we can problem solve to help our missed deadlines," and then you take Bill to lunch and berate him, you risk losing Bill's confidence forever.

When you meet with the other individual, tell him first your purpose for talking to him. Remember, Bill is searching for the what's in it for me – WIIFM component. He will be craning to see how you have his best interest at heart.

When you give someone feedback, have a respectful and sincere tone. Don't sound condescending, patronizing, parental, as if you're doing the other person a favor. Don't be angry or fearful. Be direct and respectful, and keep eye contact.

When you give feedback, be very specific with the data you are sharing. That data should include specific examples, just as you ask for specific examples when someone is giving you feedback. Instead of saying, "You just don't seem that enthusiastic about the project we're working on together," you could say, "I perceive you as not being interested in our joint project." The person asks, "Why are you saying that?"

"The reason I say that is you rolled your eyes at the last meeting and sighed loudly. Am I reading you correctly that you are tired or disinterested?"

To reiterate, state your intention up front, speak with a respectful tone and provide specific data. This will help you come across as sincere, rather than critical. Also, when you give the other person specific examples and data, you offer evidence to him that makes him accountable and the feedback becomes difficult to refute.

Let's take the example of the woman giving Cindy feedback after the seminar. Following the constructive formula to provide feedback, the woman, first, would have to ask herself why she was giving Cindy feedback. Let's suppose she wanted to help Cindy to be a better speaker. She could approach Cindy and politely say, "I've listened to you all day and would like to offer you suggestions on your presentation." Then she could say something like, "You have great enthusiasm as a speaker, and what could make you even better, in my opinion, is to adjust your tone. At times you seemed to have spoken to us as if we were children. For example, when you said . . . "

And she could have continued by saying, "I think you would have been more effective if you changed your tone to sound as though you believe we are equals. Maybe something like this. . ."

A couple of important tips:

1) Avoid the use of "but" when you are giving feedback. For example: "You are one of the most intelligent people I know, but . . . ," "You are the best looking audience, but . . ." "I don't want you to take this the wrong way, but . . ." People will always wait for the other shoe to drop, and you'll negate the first half of your statement if you use the word "but."

2) Use a technique called "perception checking" to assess how the other person is responding to you. For example, if you are giving someone feedback, and he begins looking away with a disgruntled expression, you can check with him. "Jack, it seems like you are upset with what I'm saying to you. Am I right? Keep in mind my intention is to improve our communication."

If you are giving someone feedback, and she shakes her head with a discouraged expression, you could say, "I sense you're having a hard time with this information, Katie, is that true?" In both scenarios, remember to keep your tone respectful.

How do I handle criticism?

Perception checking allows the other person to participate in the conversation and lets him know you are paying attention. Perception checking is always better than saying things like, "Jack, you roll your eyes, and you have a bad attitude. Stop it and listen to me." or "Katie, stop being so sensitive. I'm telling you this for your own good."

When you are respectful and have the other person's best interest at heart, that feedback will be beneficial for the receiver. You may still get resistance, but if your tone is sincere and you state your intention up front, you will make the information much more palatable for the person receiving your feedback.

Remember that it's important for you to paint a picture of how you see the other person now and how you would like to see his behavior modify.

Another *Eureka* for you: *The time you spend up front being consistently honest, sincere and direct with others will build a foundation of trust and reliability.* And if the time comes when you really need their help, such as a crisis, it's likely that they will be there for you. You can't expect people to rally around you when you haven't invested in them, particularly when the ship is sinking!

Applying This To You:

Giving and Receiving Feedback.

1) Recall a situation when you received feedback and reacted adversely so that it wasn't helpful to you or the other person. Rewrite here how you could react differently.

2) What specific questions could you ask? How could you paraphrase what the person said? What would you do with the information you received?

3) Think of someone to whom you need to give feedback. What will you say to that person? When will you tell him? Where?

4) What specific information will you provide?

5) Paint a picture of how you see him now and how you would like him to modify his behavior. Include his WIIFM.

6) Script how you will communicate that to him.

Chapter Nine

HOW DO I GAIN RESPECT & CREDIBILITY FROM OTHERS?

A couple of years ago, I coached a young woman named Wendy who was an administrator at a mining company. A few of the miners used profanity and inappropriate language around her, which made her feel extremely uncomfortable. Furthermore, she never quite knew what her boss expected. I asked Wendy if she had said anything about her discomfort to the miners or to her boss. She said no, because she was worried what the miners might think, and she thought her boss might fire her. Wendy was doing the best she could at the time. However, she was also helping to perpetuate the disrespectful treatment from the miners and confusion from her boss.

As part of gaining respect, it's important to set boundaries with other people at work. People won't modify their behavior until they are made aware of the need. In Wendy's case, she needed to make it known that she didn't like the miner's language and her boss' ambiguity. Wendy is going to have to go outside of her comfort zone and take a risk. She'll need to say something to the miners and her boss. If she doesn't, it's pretty certain that she'll keep getting the same behavior from them. Plus, she won't be building her communication skill base, she will diminish her self-regard, and she'll feel resentment over time.

Wendy could approach the foreman with whom she feels at ease and say, "I don't like the language you guys use, and I'd appreciate it if you don't use it around me." or "I understand you're under stress and feel relaxed with your peers; however, some of your language offends me. Would you please not use profanity around me. Thank you." This is called creating a boundary. In the long run, it will show other people that you respect yourself and expect them to do the same. On the contrary, if you do not say anything, you are tacitly letting people know that what they are doing or saying is OK with you.

She could also include *their* WIIFM (What's In It For Me) by saying, "I get distracted and offended when you guys are swearing and saying inappropriate things. I know you wouldn't like to hear other people speaking like that in the presence of your mothers, wives, daughters or sisters. I don't like it either."

If Wendy decides to speak up, there is nothing she is asking for which is unreasonable. In fact, she is creating a condition of respect for herself and others. If the miners modify their behavior, it would be good for Wendy to say, "I appreciate the effort you have made to stop swearing and using inappropriate language around me."

In regard to her boss' unclear expectations, Wendy could meet with her boss and say, "I'd like to speak with you about your perception of my role and responsibilities concerning my work. I want to make sure that we are thinking along the same lines so I can do my best work and enhance my productivity," (which includes the WIIFM for her boss.) Her manager cannot fire her for clarifying her role and responsibilities at work.

However, if she is not doing her work or not asking questions to find out what she should be doing, after time she could be let go for being an ineffective employee.

If you feel you are not getting respect, you will have to speak up, you will have to let people know what you need and what you are willing and unwilling to tolerate. You also need to be reasonable. It may be a good idea to discuss your issues with a third party or a confidante who can help make sure your request is appropriate. You may be someone who really needs to begin to treat yourself and others better. Consider asking several people you trust how they perceive your treatment of others at work. Be open to their responses. If they say your communication style is harsh, or that you don't listen or you walk on people, you need to make changes. The irony is you may be right a lot of the time regarding your ideas or your business strategies - it's the way you deal with people that needs adjusting. If you don't make changes, you will continue to show disrespect for yourself and others through your words, tone, and actions. This usually results in people's resentment and sabotage of you.

If you're trying to gain respect and credibility with others at work, here are concrete, specific actions you can take. We covered in length, in Chapter Five, how you can impact people through your tone and body language. Never is this more important than when you begin a new job and are trying to make a positive impression with people. As basic as this sounds, it is crucial: *You never have a second chance to make a first impression.*

Non-Verbals

Two non-verbal forms of communication which speak volumes about you are your handshake and your posture. Try this exercise at home. Walk by your mirror, once with slumped, rounded shoulders, and once with your shoulders back and head held high. Look at the difference between the two. How does each posture make you feel? I'll guarantee you that people will observe you in exactly the same way that you feel while watching yourself in the mirror. Practice walking with your shoulders back and your head held high - not arrogantly, but confidently. You will begin to feel more confident and people will treat you better. You will make yourself less of a target, even with the bully types.

Second, when you shake someone's hand, shake web to web, two or three pumps. Do not grab the end of their fingers. And don't hold on to the person's arm or shoulder like you're running for office. "If you vote for me, I'll make sure your kids go to college." When you shake someone's hand, look them in the eyes confidently. This style of greeting is widely accepted in western business settings, but if you are in another country, or meeting someone from another country, do some research to learn that culture's etiquette and protocol.

People will pay attention to how you present yourself. We like others who look composed and confident. This doesn't mean you're not going to have days when you feel unsure. You are. But you're trying to create a sense of credibility, and this is best done visually and non-verbally.

Check your tone and your voice volume. People who speak louder are perceived as more confident while people who speak softer are perceived as timid and uncertain. In addition, check how much space you give others around you, especially in a business setting. Remember a minimum of three feet is acceptable. Don't crowd others' personal space.

Again, ask someone who knows you and whom you trust what your tone sounds like. Is it pleasant, relaxed, confident? If they tell you that you seem tentative or unsure, that's OK. At this point, you are trying to assess and gain awareness of how you are perceived. It won't help you to be hard or judgmental toward yourself. Rather, realize you have some things to work on and then you can begin practicing to make gradual changes. Keep in mind that anyone who is very good at something has had a lot of practice honing their skills.

Early in my career, after a business meeting, I asked my manager how I sounded when I made a couple of suggestions during the meeting. He said, "Your suggestions were good, and you would even sound more credible if you spoke louder." This was very helpful feedback for me, because my voice tends to be low. Not everyone could hear me. Over time, his advice proved invaluable. You'll be surprised when you do make slight alterations, how it affects your credibility.

How do I gain respect & credibility from others?

Words

Below are examples of phrases that people commonly use at work. See how you respond to them.

> *"This probably is a stupid question, but ... "*
>
> *"I haven't been to graduate school like the rest of you, however ... "*
>
> *"... OK?" "... don't you agree?"*
>
> *"awesome" "totally" "really" "super" "like"*
>
> *"I'm sorry I haven't prepared much ... "*
>
> *"I guess it's true." "I suppose this is accurate data."*
>
> *"I kinda think this ... " "I sorta believe ... "*

The first two examples above are hedging statements: "This is probably a stupid question, but ... , " and, "I haven't been to graduate school like the rest of you, however ... " The speaker is setting people up to concentrate on the negative. If I say to you, "Gosh you're talented but ... " You're going to be looking for the flaw, right? You'll also sound defensive, so try not to make hedging comments. Rather, make declarative statements such as, "I have two ideas to improve the bottom line," or "I don't think this method will work. Let me explain why" or "The data for this report is significant. The first example is ... "

The questions "OK?" and "Don't you agree?" are all right, sometimes, but if you say them frequently, they convey uncertainty. If you add a tentative tone, you will diminish your credibility.

The expressions "totally," "awesome," "really," "super," and "like" used continuously give a sense of high school or college student speak. Again, they are OK if used infrequently, but don't make a steady diet of them.

"I'm sorry I haven't prepared much" is not a good excuse. People will rightly assume you didn't take the time or you didn't care enough to do your work.

"I guess it's true" or "I suppose the data is accurate" sounds weak. Check your information and to be sure, corroborate the information with another source.

We hear "kinda" and "sorta" constantly. Listen to the difference. "I kinda think that we should be conserving water now because of the drought" and "I sorta believe it's a good idea to get an MBA" versus "I think that we should be conserving water now because of the drought" and "I believe it's a good idea to get an MBA." The difference speaks for itself. Imagine a doctor saying to you, "I sorta think it's good for you to have an operation to avoid any future complications."

Your words are important, and your words coupled with your non-verbals and tone will determine how people perceive you. (People believe their perceptions are accurate, so you want to be aware of how you are perceived.)

Actions

You might be thinking about deeds and wondering if they account for anything. Of course they do. People's deeds go a long way in cultivating trust and credibility with others. Your actions can be measured, and there are actions you can take that will enhance your level of respect and credibility. Here are some of those specific actions.

First of all, own responsibility. See yourself as someone who contributes and is accountable for your actions, instead of someone who always blames others and who doesn't own up to your part in a situation. When you have made a mistake, you don't have to make a big deal out of it, but say you're sorry and try to make the situation better. We don't like it when people have a litany of excuses. If you goofed, admit it to others and take responsibility. You will build credibility and respect that way. Conversely, you'll damage your credibility and respect if you try to cover up or lie. Think of all the corporate executives at Enron, WorldCom, and Tyco.

Avoid gossiping about others. It can be insidious and damaging. And never forget, if they are talking about others, they're talking about you when you're not around - guaranteed.

Keep people's confidences. Someone trusted you enough to tell you important information and confide in you. If you violate that trust, it's almost impossible to get it back, and you will create an adverse reputation for yourself.

When someone gives you feedback, react appropriately. Don't just fly off the handle and react as we've discussed. You give your power away if you haven't gathered data before you respond. Also, you just might say something that you can never take back. Remember the three-hour, 3-C rule? If you feel hot about the comment, walk away for three hours and see if you think differently about it. Stay cool, composed and confident. The same goes for responding to e-mail.

Be punctual and practice business etiquette. Once I coached an individual at an organization where her peers were making excessive personal phone calls, going house shopping during business hours, and making wedding plans. Watching this, my client thought she could play, too. So, she did. She took extra time on her lunch hour, made some personal calls, etc. She was summoned into the president's office, and he said to her, "Your manager told me you're being irresponsible. Did I misjudge your character?" She launched into this long explanation about what other people were doing at the office, and he listened to her. When she finished speaking, he said to her, "Why would you want to place yourself in a group of the lowest common denominator?" To this day, I've never forgotten her story. The president's counsel is advisable to take to heart, for you or anyone who feels she should behave as the rest of the herd does.

Manage your expectations and perceptions. Don't assume other people share your expectations or have the same perceptions of a situation. Ask questions consistently and often to clarify information.

Give other people feedback when you need something from them, or you feel it would benefit them to hear what you have to say. Remember to check your intent. If the feedback is in their best interest and you give them feedback in a direct, respectful manner, they will only respect you more over time. (See Chapter Eight on Giving Feedback.) If you talk behind their backs and circumvent them, you will make them cautious and suspicious, perhaps retaliatory of you.

When you are working for an organization, it's important to build an alliance that is based on mutual trust and respect. By an alliance, I mean a network of people you can depend on and who can depend on you. This takes time. Studies indicate that it takes about seven months to develop trust with another individual at work. *People will trust you most through your actions over time.* Your actions need to be consistent and match your words. It takes less than half that time to destroy trust.

It's important for your colleagues and bosses to see you being genuine and consistent in different contexts. *Visibility is key.* You can't be visible behind your office door or staying home avoiding company events. Therefore, it's going to help you to build networks by spending time with people and showing them that you are interested and reliable and there for them if they need you. You will build credibility and respect through your professional network.

For introverts, this is going to be difficult. You probably already know if you are an introvert or not, but if you have any doubt, think about spending five days at a convention where you have activities every day and evening. Does that thought exhaust you? If so, most likely you're an introvert. This doesn't suggest introverts aren't socially skilled; they just need more private time. If you feel invigorated by the thought of spending five days at a convention, it's highly likely that you're an extrovert. Extroverts have an easier time networking than introverts do, because they are energized by interacting with people. But in either case, it's important to network for your credibility, respect and your career.

Be impeccable with your word. Do not say something if you don't think you will do it, won't do it or can't do it. The only thing you have is your word. Make sure you do what you say and say what you do.

Use humor appropriately. Humor is incredibly powerful, disarming and can diffuse tension.

Perceptions of Power.

There is an assessment called Perceptions of Power which analyzes what *you* perceive to be the source of *your power*. In other words, why are you able to get people to do what you want them to do? There are seven perceptions of power.

The first is known as the power of *position*. That means by virtue of holding a title such as vice president, director or manager, you are able to influence others.

A second perception is *reward* power. You are able to reward people at work for what you deem rewardable. You can give them a pay raise, time off, compensation time, shift trades, etc.
A third perception of power is known as *punishment* power

which is the opposite of reward power. You can punish people or impose sanctions against them.

A fourth type is called *expert* power, which means that you possess a particular body of knowledge and expertise.

The fifth perception of power is known as *connection* power. You think that you have power over others because you know certain people, are connected to people who can make things happen or who are decision makers.

The sixth perception is called *information* power. You possess information that is helpful to others in a positive or negative way. This includes gossip.

The seventh perception of power is known as *referent* power. This means you are trusted, respected and accessible to others. Referent power embodies every action in this chapter on how to gain respect and credibility. Here are the perceptions of power in a work setting. The following is a true scenario.

A vice president for a large, multibillion dollar company had an aura about her similar to Joan Collin's character from the television show "Dynasty" and Heather Locklear's character, Amanda Woodward, from the television show, "Melrose Place." Gloria drove a Mercedes Benz, had a personal shopper at Saks Fifth Avenue, owned a cell phone before they were popular, and got her nails polished every week for $100 a pop. People seemed to gravitate toward Gloria, who was also attractive.

Since Gloria was a vice president, she did have position power. She used her position power with her staff of 10 to delegate and make decisions. Gloria also had reward and punishment power, which she used at her discretion, for promotions, salary increases and giving particular assignments. She had people run errands for her and take care of her personal business at times. If they didn't, life would be difficult at work. She had connection power because she worked with other vice presidents, high-level clients and the president of the company.

Gloria began a huge campaign for the company and promoted values that included integrity and respect, impeccable customer service internally and externally. Gloria said they should all go the extra mile no matter what. She conducted corporate meetings and began to gain people's confidence and commitment to her value and customer service crusade.

However, the credibility and respect that Gloria gained over time soon began to unravel. Since she was touting honesty, people began to come to her office, in private, and speak with her about things that bothered them. As a result, Gloria had information power. However, Gloria violated confidences and began telling people what certain employees told her. Since the company had thousands of staff, Gloria was able to do this for awhile, until people realized she was betraying those confidences.

Gloria began having an affair with another employee in her office. The man would come over during the day, and they would lock her door and emerge an hour later. It may have been her idea of going the extra mile. Her employees knew it was happening, but they were afraid to say anything for fear of retaliation. Remember that Gloria had punishment power, which she did use, sometimes unjustly.

Sooner or later, people began to talk and told the president of the company of her antics. At first, he defended her, dismissing people's talk as mere gossip, but when Gloria and her beau planned a trip together to Jamaica on the company payroll, he could no longer deny the allegations. Gloria was soon dismissed from her job.

There are several lessons we can learn from this story. Many people ask me how they can gain credibility and respect with others without having the ability to hold power over people with a title or the ability to punish or reward them. Keep in mind that a title will only get you so far. There have been many people with titles who misused their position and had a negative impact on others. Even if you can reward people or punish them, those powers will only work for so long. If you are affiliated with people of prestige and status, that will only serve you to an extent. You only need think of the story of Gloria.

The two perceptions of power that have the greatest ability to garner credibility and respect are *expert* power and *referent* power. You can always read and study and gain certificates, degrees, and expand your body of knowledge. Education is a lifelong process. You may never hold an official title, but no one can ever obstruct your ability to grow. Share that knowledge with others, and you will be known as the person with information. Information is power. It will give you tremendous leverage to gain credibility and respect. You can also have referent power. Time and time again, I have meet successful people who have no titles, who are perhaps somewhat awkward with others, maybe a little shy and are not formally educated. What they do have is a great attitude and the desire to make things better for themselves and others. They constantly read and learn and maintain their sense of humor about life's challenges. They treat themselves and others with the utmost sense of respect, and they draw boundaries if necessary. If they are struggling with an issue or problem, they seek help and try to move forward proactively rather than complain incessantly.

The *Eureka* for you: *This entire book is about expanding your referent power. You are gaining confidence, problem solving, learning to be approachable, and developing the ability to work with many different people. What an opportunity you have!*

Applying This To You:

Gaining Respect and Credibility From Others.

1) With whom do you need to set a boundary? Who do you feel treats you with disrespect or like a doormat?

2) Set up a dialogue on how you will approach this person and what you will say. Refer to Wendy's story at the beginning of the chapter.

3) Are you someone who is hard on others? Do you find yourself criticizing others? If there is a reason, is your feedback harsh? Think of someone with whom you have been excessively difficult.

4) Configure a dialogue with that person. Write down your intention and ask him how you can be a better manager or co-worker to him. Watch the doors open.

5) What kind of power do you think you have? What can you specifically do to augment your expert power? How can you expand your referent power?

6) What words can you modify when you speak? Do you use any hedging words or language, which would make you appear less confident and credible? What changes can you make?

7) How is your posture and handshake? Ask someone you trust to assess both.

Chapter Ten

HOW CAN I BE A BETTER SPEAKER AND GAIN A SENSE OF CONFIDENCE?

This subject is near and dear to my heart, because it's how I make a living. I have great compassion for people who are uncomfortable speaking in public. I, too, was once so scared of people to the point of physical illness. But I also know being able to conquer your fears, particularly in a forum such as speaking, is very powerful.

According to research, speaking in front of an audience, ranked first out of all people's fears. Even above death and snakes! As Jerry Seinfeld jokes, if you're at a funeral, it's easier to be in the box than giving the eulogy.

Yet, when you are a proficient speaker, you can use this skill to gain recognition, feel more confident and poised, and earn a greater income. Do you know of one manager, director or vice president who doesn't give presentations?

Included in this chapter are three sections which include techniques for developing presentation content, delivery and preparation. If you haven't read Chapter Four on taking a risk, it will be helpful to take the time to read it before continuing on.

Let's first consider presentation content. If you separate your presentation into sections, it will be easier for you to remember and for your audience to absorb. You can use this structure for audiences or groups of any size.

The first thing to ask yourself is what do you want to achieve by giving this presentation? For example, do you want to inform people of something? Do you want to evaluate, interpret or clarify data? Do you want to motivate people? Do you want to sell an idea? What do you want to do? If you don't know your purpose, there's no way your audience will be able to figure it out. Ask yourself this question: As a result of my presentation, what do I want to accomplish? Be very specific. For example, you could say that you want to convince everyone to vote for a new healthcare plan, or you want to explain the revised sexual harassment policy, or gain management approval for a new computer software operating system.

Next, you want to know the makeup of your audience. Specifically, you want to know their backgrounds, experience, age, gender, reasons for attending (is it mandatory?), some of their concerns, some of their goals, their receptiveness to hearing you, biases about your subject, etc. You may be wondering two things: why do you need all the information on the audience, and how the heck do you gather that intelligence? You want this information because you are going to present *from their perspective*. That's right, their perspective. You are going to see things from their vantage point which will give you an advantage. Empathy is a very, very effective tool.

You can get information about your audience by talking to the person who requested you to speak. Request a list of the attendees and their titles, and study background information on the group, such as organizational charts, annual reports, and job descriptions. You can also send a questionnaire to audience members before your presentation. Prior to presenting, I like to talk to selected participants over the phone or in person. Assure them that the information will be used, and that their specific input will be confidential. Pay attention to patterns and themes with the information you collect. This will help you write your presentation content outline.

Next, formulate a general outline of your presentation. You'll add supporting information later on. Let's say your topic is dogs. Now you have to be clear on what you want your audience to get out of the presentation. Let's assume it's a persuasive presentation, and you want to convince the audience of single people that they should own a dog, because she will add years to their lives and much love and enjoyment. That's your overall premise and reason for giving the presentation.

Now that you're clear on your purpose, begin forming key points to the general outline. It's advisable to have no more than three key points every twenty minutes. Your first key point could be that dogs are great companions. Your second key point might be that they provide many health benefits. Third, dogs give you something to look forward to everyday.

You can use this general formula for any presentation. Let's say that you are trying to inform your staff about the new sexual harassment policy. Your overall purpose for talking to the group could be to help them understand the policy and the implications to them and the company. Your first key point could be to explain the law itself. The second key point could be to let them know what could happen to them if they ignore the law, and the third key point could be what could happen to the company if the law is ignored.

Now that you have your general outline, you can begin to embellish each key point with evidence or information that will support your point. Evidence takes many forms. You can use examples or graphs. You can give a demonstration or show a videotape. You can provide convincing statistics, you could give testimonials, or you could even tell an anecdote.

Let's go back to the dog speech. Your first point was that dogs make great companions. You could begin by telling an anecdote about your life with your dog, the joy of taking her for walks everyday or having her sit next to you while you pay bills. You might show a video of people happily interacting with their dogs. Believe it or not, doggy happy hours have sprung up throughout the U.S. It would be fun to show pictures of the dogs munching treats from the pretzel bowls while their human companions "networked." This could also support your point that not only do dogs make for great companions, but they lead to further social companionship.

Your next point was that dogs provide enhanced health benefits. Here, you might want to have a chart with statistics illustrating specific health benefits of having a dog. You could explain how people with dogs have lower blood pressure and tend to live longer than people without dogs. Or, you could give testimonials of people who owned dogs and exhibited better-than-average healing time after surgery. Anything you could use to reinforce the point that dogs provide enhanced health benefits would be helpful.

Your third point was that dogs give you something to look forward to everyday. You could elaborate on this point by listing the top ten reasons to wake up in the morning because of a dog. She'll get you out of bed and into a routine, she'll depend on you, she'll make you exercise and provide a social outlet at the park. You could give an example of a elderly person you know who was suicidal and decided to live after the addition of a family dog.

Follow the same format with the presentation on the sexual harassment policy. The overall purpose of the presentation is to inform your staff about the new sexual harassment policy. The first point was to tell the staff about the policy. You could provide a simple slide of the actual law. Then you can give examples to define the law: what it is, and what it isn't. You might offer evidence by bringing in samples of inappropriate pictures or jokes or ask the group to give examples.

The second point is to let the staff know what will happen to them if they don't follow the policy. You could provide evidence through actual case studies.

The last point is the implications to companies for not adhering to sexual harassment policies. Statistics as evidence would be powerful here. There are a multitude of cases available where companies have been sued millions of dollars, directly affecting the manager.

In between your main points, it's helpful to you and the audience if you provide transitions. Transitions are short, simple connectors from one point to another. They should tie your presentation together in an interesting, logical sequence.

Here are some examples:

> *"Now that we've covered why dogs are such great companions, I'm going to talk about the tremendous health benefits they offer."*
>
> *"Moving from dogs as companions, did you know that people who own dogs tend to live longer? I'm now going to discuss the health benefits of owning a dog."*
>
> *"We've discussed the implications for the company of not following sexual harassment laws, now let's discuss how that can affect your personal pocketbook."*
>
> *"Not only is the company liable, but you as managers are, too. Let's move on to your personal responsibility in regard to the law."*

After you have determined your main points and provided evidence, you can create an opening and closing to your presentation. When you open a presentation, it's important to grab your audience's attention by making it interesting. Sometimes people begin in a fumbling manner, maybe hem and haw and say something like, "Well, I've been asked to speak with you about healthcare, so I will." That's a bad beginning. Also, never apologize. For example, do not begin by saying, "I'm sorry I have a cold so forgive me if I sound nasal." or "I didn't have much time to prepare but I hope you still like it." Don't do that!

This is your opportunity to be creative. Act enthusiastic and happy that you're the one speaking and be eager to tell them what you have to say. In the dog presentation example, you could begin by saying, " If I could tell you a wonderful way to prolong your life, how many of you would be interested?" or "People have been known to live longer by having one of these in their home. Do you know what these are?"

For your presentation on sexual harassment laws, you could begin by saying, "The violation of this law costs companies billions of dollars every year. I'm going to tell you about this law, and how you can avoid litigation." or "If your personal assets were depleted by $300,000, what implications would this have on your life?"

It's a great idea to begin with a question or statistic or quotation which is relevant to the group and gets the audience's attention. Once you've gotten their attention, you're going to tell them the major areas you will be covering during your presentation. Don't worry about giving your presentation away. Redundancy is good for effect! Keep in mind that it takes the average person eight times to hear something before they get it. That's right, eight times!

Let's put this together and see what it sounds like. First, the dog presentation: People have been known to live longer by having one of these in their homes. Do you know what these are? Pause and people will answer.

"*Food.*"

You say, "*Try again.*"

They say, "*A pet.*"

You could say, "*Right, a pet. What kind?*"

They say, "*A cat.*"

You say, "*Try again. You're close.*"

They say, "*A dog.*"

You say "Right, and today we're going to talk about how owning a dog can prolong your life. Specifically, we'll discuss companionship with dogs, health benefits, and how to make your life long lasting and filled with love and joy."

The other advantage to this type of opening is you've involved the audience and engaged them through their participation. This effective strategy also takes the focus off you. That helps with the nerves.

Let's try the presentation on the sexual harassment law. You could begin with the opener, "If your personal assets were depleted by $300,000, what implications would this have on your life?" or "What if you had $ 300,000 one day, and it vanished the next when you could have prevented that from happening?"

Now you're going to tell people what you will talk to them about. "Believe it or not, this has happened to people just like you. Today, I'm going to talk to you about our new sexual harassment policy and the implications it has for our company and you, personally."

To recap so far, it's advisable to write your presentation in this order: general outline followed by your key points, your supporting evidence and then your opener.

For the last part of the presentation, you'll create an ending. Similar to the opening, this is a significant part of your presentation. It's a good idea to end with a brief summary of the information you covered, and then ask a question to get the audience thinking, or read a quote or end with an anecdote. Remember, you want to be clear on what the outcome should be for your audience. Make sure they know your purpose, too. If you don't know, they won't know.

You could end your dog speech with an endearing story about an individual and her dog, or ask the audience, "Now that you know there's a practical way to enhance your life and add love and joy, why wouldn't you add a canine family companion?"

For the sexual harassment law presentation, you might end with, "You cannot afford to ignore sexual harassment laws, can you?" or "These laws have profound implications for our company and all of us. We can all serve as role models in our positions as managers."

When you fly in a plane you most likely remember the takeoff and landing. Similarly, your audience will remember the beginning and ending of your presentation. Take the time to prepare a memorable presentation.

Next, I want to cover the delivery of your presentation. Remember, you are not alone in being hesitant or fearful about speaking. Many actors, singers and performers are anxious when going before an audience, too. On the other hand, I can't think of a more satisfying, invigorating experience. When done well, it will make you feel great. The key is preparation. You want to be extremely sure of the flow of your content, the timing of your presentation and your delivery style. There are a multitude of books on speaking and giving presentations. I'm going to offer you my summation on what makes a good delivery. You can certainly supplement this information with research on grammar usage, diction, pronunciation and other mechanical techniques.

Think about a speaker, or someone who gave a presentation, who you thought was effective. What were some of the qualities that person possessed? What did he sound like? How did he respond to you? What made him unique? I'm going to guess that you did not say he spoke in a condescending tone, or he gave complicated formulas, or he never smiled! Who do we enjoy listening to? Someone who likes his topic, respects the audience - and is able to laugh at himself. We want a speaker who is confident, yet accessible to us, knowledgeable but not arrogant, likeable but not an egomaniac.

If you consider effective historical figures who were good speakers, who comes to mind for you? Perhaps it's Eleanor Roosevelt, Martin Luther King Jr., Margaret Thatcher, or Indira Ghandi. Popular present-day people include former New York City Mayor Guliani, Oprah Winfrey and Bill Clinton. All these individuals were or are seemingly approachable, accessible, the common person's person. We like that in a speaker, too. We like humility and thoughtfulness and someone who is on our level, don't we? That persona is timeless.

For starters, when you present, be animated, expressive, and genuine! If you don't care about yourself, your audience or your topic, the audience won't either. It's that simple. Be enthusiastic and care about your topic.

Keep in mind that you are the best "prop" for your presentation. Powerpoint slides are frequently used these days, but many people merely read from their slides and have minimal audience connection. The audience reads along with them. After about 15 minutes, the presentation gets very dull and tiring. If you use powerpoint, consider limiting it to graphs and charts for which it is a great visual tool. Remember that you are the main attraction when you're speaking. You want to look good and sound interesting. Make sure you are the presentation and not the powerpoint slides.

Wear something that makes you feel comfortable and confident. You know the outfit you have that brings out the color of your eyes or compliments your build? That's the one to wear. Don't wear something that makes you feel dowdy or is pinned together. I have a friend who wore a skirt that didn't fit her well because she had lost weight. She turned to make a point and her skirt dropped to her ankles before an audience of 200. An attention grabber for sure, but not the way you want!

Once, I spoke before a group of managers at the National Archives in Washington, D.C. I was wearing a suit which had six gold, double-breasted buttons that my drycleaner, unwittingly to me, covered with aluminum foil. As I was speaking, someone yelled out, "I like your suit." I looked down, and, to my shock, four buttons were still covered with foil, and one piece of foil was lying on the floor by my shoe. I said, smiling, "You guys didn't notice this 45 minutes ago when I began speaking?" Someone retorted, "We thought it was a fashion statement." "No, no fashion statement," I replied, "Just me being me. You know, I try to be pretentious, but I have a hard time pulling it off." Well everyone just howled, which brings me to my next point.

We like to be around people who have a self-deprecating sense of humor, particularly speakers. We enjoy someone who has a sense of fun. Can you imagine if I had said, "Oh, I'm so embarrassed. You must think I'm inept." That remark would have thrown off my timing and created an awkwardness for me and the audience. If you don't make a big deal out of your mistakes, other people will be less apt to.

It is never a good idea to use sexist humor, racist humor, ethic humor or off-color humor. It's inappropriate. It doesn't work well, and you'll look foolish. And the line, "Oh, the audience just couldn't tell I was kidding" doesn't work either. What would you think if I stood up and began by saying, "There was this Italian talking to an Irishman . . . " No matter what your intent, you will set yourself back. Unsuitable humor will reflect badly on you.

On the other hand, self-deprecating humor is good because it makes us look human and approachable. In the movie, "Annie Hall," Woody Allen said, "I never wanted to belong to a club that would have me as a member." That works!

We talked about using evidence earlier in this chapter. One of the most powerful pieces of evidence you can use is the anecdote. An anecdote is a story about anything that illustrates a point. I recommend including anecdotes about yourself for several reasons. If you use a personal anecdote that you really like, you will come across livelier. Think of yourself telling the story to friends who are sitting in your living room. Anecdotes allow us to relive the experience, and when we do, we tend to use natural gestures. They also give us a break from memorization because the story is easy to recall.

Once I heard a salesperson give a presentation on a new software system to non-technical people. He began by telling his audience he was going to review the system, then he launched into a story about a time he spoke to a group of senior citizens at a community center who had no experience with computers. He continued to mention his enjoyable experience teaching a couple of participants and said by the end of the seminar, they were well-versed. A few even got part-time jobs that included computer skills. The anecdote was personal and alleviated many of the fears of the people to whom he was speaking. He also was conveying to them that they were in good, confident hands.

Audiences find anecdotes interesting. As a speaker, you will discover that using a favored, appropriate anecdote will make you more animated. Wouldn't you rather listen to someone tell a suspenseful or humorous story than have them read from their powerpoint notes?

Many people ask me about using gestures. There are various schools of thought on gestures. I encourage you to use your natural gestures. Gestures help the audience "see" what you're talking about; however they must be natural, not contrived. When President Carter was in the White House, the experts tried to choreograph his movements, and he looked ridiculous because his gestures appeared forced.

Ask people to give you feedback about your gestures when giving a presentation, videotape yourself, or use a mirror while rehearsing your presentation. Watch to see if you do anything distracting, like play with change in your pocket or fumble with your jewelry. Some people have the habit of pacing back and forth on the stage like a panther at the zoo or rocking in place. Those are not gestures. Those are annoying habits.

Gestures should be purposeful. Rocking in place and moving your hands through your hair are not purposeful. Using your hands or arms to act something out, recreate a memory, or demonstrate something are gestures that are interesting. Even something as simple as holding a prop can be effective. For example, if you're giving a presentation about credit cards, having a credit card to show the audience is more interesting to watch than no credit card at all.

Pointing to a prop is a useful gesture. When explaining a point, acting surprised, happy or confused is a facial gesture and can work well.

Preparation is essential and critical. Have you ever been in a school play or performed musically or in a sport? Most of us have. What would have happened if you didn't practice or had dress rehearsal or just showed up the day of the event to participate? I'm always amazed at people who don't prepare, who just get up to speak and wing it. If you work that way, you can set yourself up for an unpleasant experience. It's also an insult to your audience because they have invested time to come hear you, and you want to give them the very best presentation you can.

Try this: Write an outline of your presentation including your opener, main points, supporting evidence and closing. Then begin to rehearse by practicing the opening until you have it down cold. Proceed to your first main point and evidence. Practice speaking out loud from the opening of the presentation through the main point and evidence. When you have that section in your mind, go to your second main point and evidence and start over from beginning through the first main point and evidence and through the second main point and evidence.

The only part I suggest you memorize is your opener. It's so important that you know the first part of your presentation by heart because that will give you confidence and also serve to move you to your first main point. For the remainder of your presentation, you can recall concepts or main points, but you don't have to memorize it word for word.

To reiterate, after the opener, tell the audience what you're going to talk about. Remember that it allows the audience to know exactly what to expect. It also gives you a clear recipe to follow.

Practicing *out loud* will make a huge difference for you. If you don't do this, your presentation will sound foreign to you when you are finally "live" in front of people. At first, it may sound strange to practice alone, out loud, but after a few times, you will begin to sound natural. As you practice, you will also increase your confidence level, significantly, and then you begin to *own* your presentation. That's a good thing. Practice and then practice on another day. You want to feel like you can't go through it anymore because you cannot present it any better.

Now you're ready to give your presentation.

I can't emphasize enough that *preparation* and *practice* is essential to a successful presentation. You might be thinking, yes, but I know my topic well. And I say to you, that's great. Keep in mind that it's different knowing your presentation in your head versus communicating your topic effectively before an audience.

The *Eureka* for you: *Practice, practice*, and *practice* some more until you feel you can't practice anymore. *Then* you will be ready to deliver your presentation.

It's also better to know too much information than too little, because you want to be prepared to answer any audience questions. Never make up an answer. I'm sure you've heard this before, and the best thing to say is, "I don't know" or "I'm not sure but I will check and let you know." And then follow through. You will learn something and gain trust with that person. Repeat the question to the person to make sure you heard the question correctly, and the rest of the audience understands the question before you respond. When you repeat the question, you will have time to gather your thoughts and decide how you will respond.

Applying This To You:

Structure a Brief Presentation.

Purpose: At the end of my presentation my audience will be able to _____

1) Opening

Today, I'll talk to you about _____

2) Main Point # 1

    A. Evidence

    B) Evidence

3) Main Point # 2

    A) Evidence

    B) Evidence

4) Main Point # 3

    A) Evidence

    B) Evidence

5) Closing

Chapter Eleven

HOW DO I KNOW WHEN IT'S TIME TO LEAVE A SITUATION, JOB OR RELATIONSHIP?

In the 1970's, David Ruffin, formally with the Temptations, released a comeback hit called "Gonna Walk Away From Love," which includes these poignant lines: *"It's not that I don't love you, you know how much I do. It's just a feeling that builds inside me . . . so I'm leaving, I'm leaving, yes I am . . . I'm gonna walk away from love, before love breaks my heart . . . "*

How do you know when to stay in a situation or leave? This is a common question especially concerning work, a friendship or romantic relationship. Consider these scenarios. Your boss makes you half-crazed with her unreasonable requests and humiliating outbursts. Friends only call you when they need something, don't keep commitments and seem to drop you for better offers. Love relationships have you confused, off-balance and with diminished self-respect. Do these sound familiar? How many times have you been in a position where you didn't know whether to hang in there or cut your losses and get out?

No one person can tell you what you should do about your personal situation. I can give you advice, and your neighbor can give you advice, and your mother can give you advice, and so on. However, you are the only one who has the right answer for you. You have to look into your heart and ask yourself if the situation is giving you what you *need*. Is the payoff greater than the emotional, physical, mental, and spiritual costs? Does this person or job "feed" you and give you what you need? Do you feel nourished, energized and good about the situation? Maybe you feel perpetually discouraged or ill with headaches, backaches, and anxiety because of the circumstances. Only you can answer that.

In addition to following your heart, there are *concrete steps* you can take to help you evaluate what action is best for you. Keep in mind that we don't have control over another's behavior. We delude ourselves into thinking that we do, but we don't. Usually people do what they want because they have learned to do those things, they are unaware of their effect on others, or they don't know differently. However, we *do* have control over our *choice* of how to react to others and whether to stay or leave.

A good place to begin is to ask yourself, what do *you need* from a friendship, relationship or job? Make a *specific* list. Don't think of the job you're in now or a particular relationship. At this point, you are making a subjective list of what you need to make you feel fulfilled in a specific area of your life. Also, don't worry about what other people would think about your list. It is *your* list. For example, list what *you* would *need* to make your work enjoyable. In a way, you're listing your "best of all worlds" job or relationship. Be realistic, too. If you say, "I'd like all people to be exactly like me," or as a woman said to me one time, "I'd like to have people stop asking dumb questions," it's obviously not going to happen.

Perhaps you need a boss who gives you clear direction or a manager who gives you feedback regularly on your work performance. Put that on your list. The same goes for friendships and relationships Make a list of what you would need to make it worthwhile. Clarify *specifically* what you need from those individuals or that job. Your list may include: I need him to be good-natured, or I need her to be reliable. It's important to be honest and clear on your list. Include both your emotional and practical needs. What you need to make you feel good. What do you need to support yourself?

After you complete your list, circle the top three most important items on your list. These three should be your non-negotiable items. Under any circumstances you will not compromise them. For instance, let's say your job list includes the following:

- 60k salary per year
- Challenging work that is not routine
- The latest technological office equipment
- Clear vision of a career path
- Short commute
- Academic environment
- Bright office space
- Family benefits
- Frequent feedback from your boss
- Friendly co-workers

From your need list, decide on your top three non-negotiable items.

From this example, let's say they are:

1) 60k per year (to meet your expenses)
2) Challenging work that is not routine (to keep you motivated)
3) Family benefits (because you have two young children at home)

Now, rank the importance of the rest of your items from your master list. Use this point system: 1 (not as important) to 10 (extremely important.) The other items on the list such as commute, the bright office space, clear vision of a career path, etc., are negotiable. There is flexibility with the other seven items on your list. Rank the remaining items from 1 to 10. Pretend you ranked the items as follows:

| Job Needs | Rank from 1 (not as important) 10 (extremely important) |

60k per year — non-negotiable
Challenging work that is not routine — non-negotiable
Family benefits — non-negotiable
The latest technological office equipment — 8
Clear vision of a career path — 5
Short commute — 7
Academic environment — 9
Bright office space — 8
Frequent feedback from your boss — 6
Friendly co-workers — 9

You can clearly see from your need list, the top three items which are non-negotiable and the remaining items which are flexible to varying degrees.

Next, take a look at a tool known as the Decision Making Chart. This chart will help you to list the job, friendship or relationship needs most important to you and then determine if those needs are being meet. Let's stay with the job example.

1) *List your job needs in the left column, as illustrated on the following page, beginning with your three non-negotiable items.*

2) *Include all your possible options at the right so you can compare your needs list from the left-hand column with your possible options.*

3) *Consider each option as compared to your need list. Is the need being met? If it is, write yes in the corresponding space. If not, write no, or you don't know. If your response is you don't know, then you need to get more information.*

Job Needs	All possible options (can be as many as you like)	
	Your current job	*job choice # 2*
60k salary (non-negotiable)	60k	62k
Challenging work/not routine (non-negotiable)	yes	yes
Family benefits (non-negotiable)	ok	ok
The latest technological office (8) *equipment*	no	yes
Clear vision of career path (5)	no	yes
Short commute (7)	yes	no
Academic environment (9)	yes	yes
Bright office space (8)	yes	no
Frequent feedback (6) *from your boss*	no	don't know
Friendly co-workers (9)	no	don't know

Analyze your responses. Pay particular attention to your options as compared to your three non-negotiable items. If one of the options *does not* meet your non-negotiable needs, then that option is eliminated, *or* you'll have to make your need item(s) negotiable in order to keep the choice. Either way, this process will direct and focus you as to what would be the best decision for you.

Viewing this chart, both options meet the non-negotiable needs on your list.

Follow the same procedure for all your options, rating each option against your needs list, keeping in mind that with some items you have more flexibility than with others.

Look for the gaps between what you put on your needs list and what you perceive you are getting from the job, prospective job, friendship or relationship. Remember, focus on what you ranked as most important to you on your need list in the left-hand column. You scored the next highest needs as: the latest technological equipment and bright office space (8 each), academic environment and friendly co-workers (9 each.)

According to the chart, you do have the latest technological equipment with choice number # 2 but not in your current job; however, you do have bright office space in your current job, but not in your second job option. That would be a trade-off for you. You would have an academic environment in both options. The next area of interest to you is friendly co-workers. You don't have friendly co-workers in your current job, and you don't know if co-workers are friendly in job choice # 2. It would benefit you greatly to find out more information about job choice # 2, since you ranked friendly environment as a 9.

The beauty of the Decision Making Chart is that it provides you with a clear visual graph of where your needs are being met, areas to be negotiated and places to find out more information. In a prospective job opportunity, you often need to interview your prospective employer sufficiently to find out about areas such as technology, frequency of management feedback, job growth, etc. This will help you complete your chart optimally.

What if you had given "receiving feedback from your boss" a ranking of 9? Feedback, of course, would be important to you. Before you leave a job or relationship, you want to make sure that you have done everything possible to communicate your needs to the other person. If you haven't, that would be a good next step. As we talked about earlier, no one can read your mind. It may be helpful to review Chapter Seven, "How Do I Get What I Want?", at this juncture. The chapter will give you ideas on how to approach people in a proactive, positive way. If you're not communicating what you need currently in your job or relationship, it's pretty much a given that you won't in a new job or relationship, either.

If you are in a job that you don't enjoy, perhaps you need to begin a plan to move to another department, field or industry. In that case, it might be helpful to reread Chapter Four, "You Must Be Willing To Take A Risk." It will give you ideas on how to make that happen.

A *Eureka* for you: *you always have choices, and you can make decisions which will make you happier! Sure, it's risky, but it's risky, too, if you don't choose. It's better to take the chance and make a measured, intelligent decision than to just let life happen to you.*

Consider the case of Tom, who at 50 was laid off by a high tech firm. He said he hated his job anyway, and the severance gave him time to think. He also told me, "I'm embarrassed about this, but to tell you the truth, I've always wanted to sell cars." I could see his eyes light up, and all of a sudden he came to life as he began describing cars, models and nostalgic memories. But then he began to slump down in his chair. He added that people in Washington, D.C., where he lived, were into status, titles and money.

I looked at him and asked, "Would selling cars make you happy?" Again, he perked up and responded, unequivocally, "Oh, yes." "Haven't you paid your dues by living someone else's life?" He gave another resounding, "Yes." I said, "From what you just told me and the enthusiasm that you exude, it seems you're the only one standing in your way."

Tom got a job interview with an auto superstore around

Washington, D.C. About a month after he accepted the job offer as a salesman, he called to tell me that he had broken every sales record at his new place of employment. He was even in line for a regional management position.

Another *Eureka* for you: *If you don't feel nourished and gratified in your work or in a relationship, and you've done everything you can, it is time to move on. Only you can make that decision, and make it happen.*

Sometimes it's not as simple as the example of Tom. Sarah had been seeing Henry for five months. She found Henry very attractive and charming, talented and successful, smart and funny. One item on Sarah's relationship list states that she needs to be with someone who is predictable and consistent.

Sarah's concern is that Henry is inconsistent in his behavior toward her. Sometimes he acts as if he really enjoys her company, and sometimes he is withdrawn and disinterested, causing Sarah to feel insecure, unsure and distrustful of Henry.

Sarah has discussed her feelings with Henry, and he says that he needs time to understand why he acts the way he does. His feels himself distancing, but doesn't know what to do about it. Sarah knows that Henry's last relationship was very painful for him. She is compassionate, but she doesn't want to feel anxious any longer.

Maybe you can relate to Sarah's dilemma. Does she leave Henry now and cut her losses, or emotionally invest herself further and take a risk? There is no easy answer. Only Sarah knows how much she can tolerate given the circumstances.

There are many ways to solve a dilemma like this. Sometimes putting a time limit on a situation can help. Let's say that Sarah lets Henry know that if he is still inconsistent after one year, that she will have to move on. Maybe they could go see a counselor together. Perhaps Henry needs to take time to himself for awhile. Or Sarah needs to lower her expectations.

The practice of making a list of all the pros and all the cons and counting which one is longer is a tried and true method. How many people do you know who have a list of 45 things they don't like about another person or job, but make no effort to make changes. As a result, they end up in the same place year after year.

A woman in a recent self-empowerment seminar said that she had a friend who only called her to talk about herself. She felt her primary role for her friend was that of a pseudo-therapist. I asked her if she had spoken to her friend about her feelings, and she said that she hadn't because she didn't want her friend to be mad at her. I asked what she felt she got out of the friendship, and she said that she felt needed. She added that the gap for her in the relationship was that it seemed too one-way.

If you're in a situation that feels unbalanced, ask yourself if it's a problem. If it is, have you given the other person every opportunity to know how you feel and what you need in the friendship to make it work for you?

The woman in the seminar also said she had a "helper" role as a child in her family, so she was used to being of assistance to people. I told her that it was OK to be of assistance to her friends, but that she should feel her friends are of assistance to her, too.

We should feel safe, secure and empowered through our affiliation with others. If not, something is out of balance with the friendship that inevitably will lead to resentment on the part of the one who is always giving.

One thing is for sure: you have to be clear on what it is you need, be willing to negotiate and communicate that need to the other person.

Try: "What I want from you is _____. Do you feel you can give this to me?"

If the response is "no" then you have to ask yourself if you want to stay in the situation. If the answer is, "I don't know," what needs to happen to close the gap? Perhaps you can negotiate or lower your expectations. Sometimes our expectations are just too high or unrealistic.

On occasion, it's advisable to seek outside help from a counselor, social worker, or therapist. There are a multitude of people available to you. If money is a concern, ask if your company has an Employee Assistance Program (EAP) or call a local Community Health Resources Center.

There are two more questions to ask yourself when you're deciding to stay in a job or leave it. The first question is: do I think I could return to this relationship or type of job at a later time, or would it be better to try this other option because it will be more difficult to obtain at a later date?

About eight years ago, after I finished my doctorate, I was faced with the decision to teach at a private college or continue working in the business world. I opted to teach, because it is so difficult to get an academic appointment and easier to secure a business position. After a couple of years, I realized I was going into debt. I was taking out loans so I could teach, which made no sense! So, I went back to the business sector.

You may think that taking the teaching position was unwise on my part. To this day, even though I incurred debt, I think it was the best thing I could have done. I loved teaching and plan to go back some day. In fact, I plan to retire to teaching!

The second question is: how will you feel when you're 70 years old and looking back at your life? This sounds like such a deep question, but it helps the evaluation process.

Maybe you love your work, but have an unruly boss. Or maybe you like your boss, but don't feel challenged in your work. Nothing is perfect, ever. And when we jump from job to job or relationship to relationship, we often trade one set of problems for another. That's why I'm suggesting that you look within yourself. What is it that gives you joy in your work and personal life?

Do your relationships make you feel good about yourself? Are you free to express yourself? Do you have to censor your interests and needs? Do you feel safe and secure emotionally, physically, mentally, psychologically and spiritually? Do you have fun?

The key is to know what you want from your work and from others and make that manifest as best you can. If you have done everything you can to make it happen, and you've given it a fair amount of time, but it's still not right for you, then it's probably in your best interest to move forward to something or someone who will give you what you need.

A good friend of mine told me about a simple, yet effective, decision making strategy. It works best when you are deciding between two things rather than several options. You'll need a coin of any kind. Thinking of your two decisions, designate tails for one decision and heads for the other decision. Throw the coin in the air and see where it lands. There, your decision is made for you. Consider this a permanent decision. How do you feel about it? Do you have any reservations? If your stomach is queasy because of the decision, it doesn't feel right, or you now want to flip the coin for the best two out of three, you can be sure you don't feel equally about the two options. This method has never failed me.

Applying this to you:

Make a decision.

1) Create a decision making chart for a job or relationship (follow the example at the beginning of the chapter)

2) Ask yourself these questions:

   a) Are your non-negotiables being met?
   b) Where *can* you negotiate?
   c) Can you lower your expectations?

3) Flip a coin considering your two decisions. How do you feel?

4) Formulate a plan of action to get what you need (see Chapter Four.) This may include moving on from a job or relationship.

EPILOGUE

I love to tell this story of my father, who has been one of the most influential people in my life. My father grew up impoverished, was working at eight years old and endured many hardships. He struggled enormously.

In tenth grade he dropped out of high school. His principal called him to his office and told my father, "You will never amount to anything."

My father entered the army when he was eighteen years old, during World War II. He told me while he was in the service he felt like he was on vacation because he got to sleep in until 5:00 a.m. Back home he had to get up at 4:00 a.m. to begin chores. He also began to think that he was at least half as smart as the officers, and after awhile he thought he was as smart as the officers. He began to develop a sense of self and self-confidence.

When he left the service, he was very motivated. He went back to school and got his GED, bachelor's, master's and doctorate degrees. He began his career as a music teacher and eventually became a principal and district superintendent.

My father retired a few years ago as CEO of the New York State Teacher's Retirement System in Albany, New York. When he began his position, assets were $1 billion, and when he left his position, assets were $50 billion.

My father embodies a Cinderella story. He toiled. He was given no favors or free rides. He had to learn the same things that you are working on: to be confident, to be a good speaker, to be able to understand and confront others, and to problem solve.

My parting words to you are: stay on your path, know that you can strengthen and acquire new skills that will move you forward in a direction that truly liberates you and makes you feel empowered. Listen to your own voice. Be positive and surround yourself with others who encourage you to be the best you that you can be. I support you 100% in your efforts.